THINKING
ABOUT
GOD

A THOUGHTFUL APPROACH
TO THE CHRISTIAN FAITH

J. Stanley McQuade

PORTORA PRESS
DALLAS, TX

Lord, I am not trying to make my way to your height,
for my desire is in no way equal to that,
but I do desire to understand a little of your truth
   which my heart already believes and loves.
I do not seek to understand so that I may believe,
   but I believe so that I may understand;
     and what is more,
I believe that unless I do believe I shall not understand.

Opening prayer from Anselm's Proslogion

Copyright © **J. Stanley McQuade** 2015

All rights reserved. No part of this book may be reproduced or transmitted in any form or by any means, electronic or mechanical, including photocopying, recording, or by any information storage or retrieval system, without the permission in writing from the publisher.

Cover image © Kimscreativehub | Dreamstime.com
– Moses And The Burning Bush

Published by
Portora Press, Dallas, TX

ISBN-13: 978-0692329849

Contents

	Introduction	1
I	Thinking about Thinking	3
II	Thinking about the Bible	14
III	Thinking about God	28
IV	Thinking about Jesus the Christ	34
V	Thinking about the Holy Spirit	50
VI	Thinking about Man, Sin, and Salvation	55
VII	Thinking about the Church	65
VIII	Thinking about the Sacraments	80
IX	Thinking about Worship	87
X	Thinking about the Christian Life	94
XI	Thinking about the Last Things	108

Introduction

This book is intended to introduce the interested lay person to a thoughtful approach to the Christian faith. To some believers it may appear that this exercise is unnecessary, that you either believe or you do not. The Christian faith after all is mysterious if not miraculous. I understand this point of view but I cannot rest with it. There is mystery in faith just as there is mystery in all areas of life. But there is also reason, the gift that each of us is given in some good measure. We use reason to reflect on our life and circumstances and with it hope to come to reasonable conclusions about what we should do and where we should be headed. This book is laid out accordingly. The first chapter discusses what we mean by reason and how we should go about thinking about the important matters of the faith. The following chapters discuss the Bible, God, Jesus, the Holy Spirit, the Church, and all the other important topics deriving therefrom. The basic premise throughout is that rational thinking is important in all these areas, that indeed it is indispensably necessary. By *rational thinking* I mean the weighing and comparing of the possible views on these topics so as to see which of them is the most plausible and adequate.

The theoretical background to this evaluative approach is *modern linguistic logic* built on mathematical *game theory* (which is discussed more fully in an appendix to the first Chapter). I see it as a form of *horizontal thinking*, which broadly goes about its task by judging competing explanations side by side. This horizontal approach is used in every chapter to deal with the issue at hand. This strategy can be contrasted to *vertical logic*, such as it is represented by Aristotle, which starts with some (hopefully) true basic principle and argues down from there to a conclusion. This vertical method will be discussed in chapter one where its limitations will be visible. It will not therefore be used throughout the book as a whole.

The source of all Christian teaching is ultimately the Bible; so here you will find Biblical theology and lots of it. Every topic studied begins and ends with the Biblical perspective. The Scriptures though, do not present us with an unthinking dogma or relevant statements on all matters that simply need to be located and then believed. Faith, like everything else, has a rational side and, it is submitted, a very appealing rational side. The chapters are meant to present the basic teaching of the Bible in a thoughtful manner. In representing my own perspective on these matters I readily concede that not everyone will agree with me on everything, though I dare to hope that most of what I say will be found reasonable and helpful.

I had originally planned to add appendices to each chapter to provide further information to the interested reader. This was to include such things as a discussion of modern language logic and game theory (in Chapter I); the doctrine of the Trinity, found in the Chapter on God; and a review of Darwinian evolution in connection with the Biblical doctrine of creation. These sections have instead been incorporated into the body of the book, and are generally to be found toward the end of each chapter. If you find these sections heavy going feel free to skip them and go on to the next chapter.

Finally, I have appended to each chapter suggestions as to further reading on the topic just discussed. These are not intended to be fully bibliographic by any manner but are meant to provide helpful materials for the interested reader to follow up on. Given that the internet is often now the first port of call for much of the information we seek out, I have also tried to offer an assessment of what the interested reader may come across on the web. Some of the online recommendations therefore are in regard to the contents of particular Wikipedia pages and articles as they stand at the time of this book's going to press. The reader will also find in the suggestions a healthy dose of readings still available in print, and a good number of these reflect an earlier period of scholarship. One advantage of such works is that they introduce us to an outlook unaware of current concerns and preoccupations which itself can lead to a broader perspective and grasp of those teachings at the very heart of the Christian faith.

I
Thinking about Thinking

Some Basic Notions about Faith and Reason

It always puzzled me as a young person that the most committed and enthusiastic Christians seemed to have thought very little or only superficially about their faith; whereas the thoughtful ones never seemed very enthusiastic. Faith and reason did not seem to go well together, and this should not be so. Plato recited an old fable about the statues of the great sculptor Daedalus, which were so lifelike that after you had purchased them they flew back to their maker to be sold again. This system worked well until one crafty purchaser nailed the statues to the floor. Plato's comment was to suggest that beliefs are like these statues, they tend to disappear unless you nail them down with good reasons.

The scriptures tell us always to be ready to give an account of the faith that is in us, in 1 Pet 3:15–18, and Christians down through the ages have responded to this challenge, and have generally out-thought their opponents and critics. There is a great need for this kind of thinking today, for the world in general and our culture in particular has tended to conclude that Christian belief is, at best, doubtful with not much going for it. Unfortunately the Church in general and our lay members in particular have been slow to challenge this view and take up the cudgels for the faith. And this is sad, for there is a great deal to be said on its behalf; the Church has a very strong case if we choose to stand up and make it. This book is designed to make this case and encourage us to take a more positive approach to communicating our Christian faith to the secular world around us.

But a building must have a sound foundation and some foundational questions must be answered before we begin. How you travel after all depends on where you start, and our basic assumptions and notions can either help or hinder progress. There are in fact a couple of assumptions that have often been adopted that have not been helpful.

First among these is the notion that faith does not need an intellectual foundation, that it is something that can exist on its own. We are told, for instance, that no one was ever brought into the faith by argument. This may often be the truth, but it is at best only a half-truth; for it is also true that few people, if any, come to faith *without* thinking. Most of us would not be believers today if someone had not helped us with our doubts and questions. We might even say that if God had not wanted us to think about our faith He would not have put heads on us and that a turnip would have done just as well.

A second, and an equally harmful assumption, is one that we have inherited from the ancients. It is seeing reasoning as providing "proof." This "proof" style of reasoning has come down to us from Aristotle's syllogism, that way of arguing from major premise to conclusion in a manner such as this,

> All men are mortal (major premise)
> Socrates is a man (minor or factual premise)
> So Socrates is mortal (the conclusion)

This model of reasoning almost inevitably leads to doubt, especially in religious matters, for it invites us to question either the starting point (the major premise) or the deductions we have made from it. Aristotle, of course, was well aware that the syllogism was not all that could be said about reasoning. However, such has been his prestige, that it has widely been deemed to be the essential form of valid thinking, meaning that attempts are repeatedly made to squeeze any and all arguments into this form. In this sense it is like the famous bed of the giant Procrustes that fitted everybody; if they were too tall he cut them down a bit and if they were too short he stretched them as needed. This way of going about making a case is still followed today by too many people who know very little about Aristotle, but whose influence in their thinking lives looms large. It has not been helpful in a number of areas, including that of science and it certainly merits little by way of thanks from religion. There are inevitably two problems with it. First, as was already mentioned, how do you know that your starting point, the major premise, is true? A second problem is, can you be sure that your arguments deriving from it are sound?

Set in these terms almost every argument is bound to be questionable. Take the argument from design for the existence of God (the teleological argument). This is generally acknowledged to be a most powerful argument, like finding a watch in the desert and concluding that there must have been a watchmaker somewhere. But the argument is weakened by putting it in syllogistic form. For the major premise, namely that design presupposes a designing intelligence, is obviously not always true. If you throw a pebble into a pond a beautiful multi-circular form is created, but not by a designing intelligence. More modernly, the entire Darwinian version of the development of design in living creatures is built not on intelligent design but on random genetic variations which are weeded out by the environment (the survival of the fittest). There is no need for a designing intelligence. And the teleological argument proceeding from the first principle is likewise doubtful, for we have in nature not only wonderful designs but also some that are less than wonderful. We see giant waves and exploding volcanoes wiping out villages and killing thousands of people. On television too we see hyenas pulling down and devouring newly born deer; not a pretty sight. So the teleological argument appears weak and inconclusive. All such arguments are attacked by proceeding is to find flaws of one sort or another and assume that the entire argument is false. A good example of this is to ask what God was doing through eternity before the creation of the universe. We don't know; but the problem is not made any easier by taking God out of the picture, for we must then ask where the original little ball of condensed matter come from before creation. We do not get very far by adding up the pluses and minuses of the different theories. A better method must be devised, and then taken.

Better models of thinking are indeed available. There have been major changes in thinking about logic and reasoning in the last half century or so, which, unfortunately, have not penetrated much into religious thinking. Thoughtful mathematicians, reflecting on the foundations of their trade, came up with *game theory*.[1] This is the notion that thinking is most like playing board games, such as chess, where we have pieces (the kings, queens, bishops, knights, rooks and pawns) each with permitted manoeuvres that the rules dictate they can make. Arithmetic, as another example, uses numbers and formal moves (like addition, subtraction, multiplication, and division, etc.), and this can be contrasted with algebra, on the other hand, which manipulates letter symbols.

These techniques associated with game theory, and deriving from mathematics, have since been applied to every kind of field of thinking, and in so doing have utilized all manner of symbols, moves, and manoeuvres. Our understanding of the physical sciences has benefitted a great deal from our applying these mathematical games of numbers and letters to physical systems such as electricity or the structure of atoms. Discrepancies and differences in explanations and predictions are handled by comparing and adapting alternative games until the one that fits best is settled on.

Game theory can also be applied to other fields of learning. It has been adopted to legal systems by using "word games" as well as to historical studies where so called "story games" are employed. The way conclusions are arrived at in all these fields is indeed the way that we reason about most things, and that is by comparing one solution with another until we find what we consider to be the best fit. And it is certainly the most helpful way to think about our religious beliefs, including matters related to the reality and existence of God.

Thomas Huxley, during the debate on Darwin's theory of evolution, is credited (rightly or wrongly) with the argument that if you gave a typewriter to each of a million monkeys and they each tapped one key every second, sooner or later one of them would type the complete works of William Shakespeare. Huxley, or whoever made this argument, never thought it through entirely at the time it seems. Others have done so since using probability theory which builds on simple facts such as if you toss a coin into the air there is one chance in two that it will land with either

---

[1] See especially here Gottlob Frege and his work (1840–1925).

heads or tails uppermost.² The odds against one of the monkeys typing even one line of Shakespeare's sonnet ("Shall I compare thee to a summer's day") are astronomical, and in the region of one chance in over 10^{200}. This is as near to impossibility as you can get if we consider that there have only been 10^{80} seconds since the "big bang" of creation.³ This only puts in logical form what most of us intuitively conclude, namely that the chances of a random accidental creation of the complex world as we know it are remote to the point of being ridiculous. It would be like a rubbish heap being struck by lightning and producing a Boeing 727. These sorts of reasons then, are why many physicists have abandoned the idea of an accidental creation and adopted some form or other of intelligent design. Antony Flew (1923–2010), a notable English philosopher and a forceful proponent of atheism throughout his career, caused quite a stir by abandoning his atheistic commitments in 2004. Flew came to know C. S. Lewis while they were both at Oxford, and had a great deal of respect for him, though incredibly he was unmoved by Lewis' *Mere Christianity*. He cites works such as Richard Swinburne's *Is There a God?* as having a greater impact in his case.⁴

From a variety of perspectives then, and viewed in a more appropriate logical framework, the idea of an accidental creation thus appears as an extremely low probability option. And further, when we consider the complexity of even the simplest of living creatures the notion of design becomes even more compelling.⁵ If we go on to consider such things as mind and thought, moral goodness and religion, the idea of intelligent design becomes even more forceful and we can conclude that the things we see all around us are not here by accident but are the result of an intelligent agent's purpose.

---

² You can follow out this in more detail in David Foster. *The Philosophical Scientists* (New York: 1993).

³ Estimates vary but it is still a finite length of time with 10^{80} at the upper end of the scale.

⁴ See the suggestions for further reading at the conclusion of this chapter for the details on these titles.

⁵ The odds against the accidental production of the fruit fly, a very simple organism, are estimated to be in the region of 10^{2002}!.

The same approach of comparing different explanations to find the best fit, will be taken in the chapters that follow, when we come to consider the doctrines of God and creation, the divinity of Jesus Christ, and Christian beliefs about the resurrection and other topics. This change of logical format, it will be argued, changes these notions from doubtful to convincingly probable.

Logics—Old and New

Logic studies valid forms of reasoning and, as we've already seen, the sort of arguments and assumptions we consider as valid goes a long way to determining where we end up when we come to consider serious matters. It is worthwhile then, detaining ourselves a short while longer to be sure the decks are clear before we press on. Still influential studies in this area, we noted, were carried out long ago by the classical Greek philosophers, especially Aristotle. Aristotle's logic, you'll recall, was based on the syllogism and some situations didn't fit this scheme too well.

In the nineteenth century a number of improvements were made in the arena of formal logic. It was seen, for instance, that logic and mathematics were essentially the same kind of thing. George Boole, a Professor at the University of Cork, Ireland, was able to transform the syllogism into both algebraic and arithmetical forms.[6] This link with mathematics was made even more explicit with the development of symbolic logic of the sort where "If A then B" is "Cab" and so forth. But it was all basically the same kind of reasoning, only substituting symbols for words and adding in some functions, and all this represented progress in the field.

Linguistic philosophy, or the logic and language movement, made more radical changes. This, like the Greek logics before it, began with philosophical mathematicians thinking more carefully about what they were doing and the processes they employed. The classical Greek philosophers, like Plato and Aristotle, were of the opinion that when they were talking about numbers and geometrical shapes they were talking about truly

---

[6] The results could be a little peculiar, for instance in Boole's arithmetic logic 2+2=2, but stay the course with me a little longer here.

real things. The visible entities on paper that they were working with, somehow represented real things (forms) existing in an intellectual world which could not be "seen" but only apprehended by thinking. They were therefore known as *realists*. The opposing school of thought (some have been Irish monks) said that these mathematical entities were only really names and not real things. This group were termed *nominalists*. But generally when the realists, such as Platonists, put the question to the nominalists, "names of what?", the nominalists have had great difficulty in answering, and this has had the effect of silencing the nominalists somewhat. Modern mathematicians in the latter part of the nineteenth century, and earlier here we mentioned Gottlob Frege's contribution, took a different approach to answer or skirt this problem, regarding mathematics as essentially like a board games with pieces and rules for moving them around like in the game of chess. Arithmetic then was seen as a game where the pieces are the numbers and the rules, or permissible moves, were functions such as plus (+), minus (-), multiplication (x), and division etc. Frege's key observation was that language could also be viewed in this way, the symbols being words. An obvious example here is grammar, where the words are put together in sentences using various rules, but Frege pressed beyond what he termed as "surface logic" since he was more interested in the uses of language for other purposes such as communication, logical and moral argument and the like.

His young friend Ludwig Wittgenstein, an Austrian engineer who became interested in philosophy, took up these ideas and advanced the logic of language in several ways. Wittgenstein initially took the purpose of language to be referring to things such as horses and houses. Reflecting on this he developed the idea that you got the meaning of a word by showing how you would demonstrate the existence of the thing signified to someone who doubted it. From this he concluded that the meaning of a word is reached by considering what you would do or say if someone doubted that the thing existed. If you could do this you knew what the word meant; otherwise the word was meaningless, just sounds with no meaning attached to them, like grunts. Philosophical and theological discourse on this sort of analysis was therefore not only doubtful, but could not even be spoken about in any meaningful way. Philosophical questions, according to this view, were created by misunderstandings of the logic of language, especially of the ways in which general (not particular) nouns related to their objects. This view was known as *logical positivism* and was very popular in particular with philosophers who were skeptical about metaphysical and theological notions.[7] Wittgenstein later, after further reflection and conversations with friends, modified his ideas to some extent, holding that while such things as music, poetry, aspects of philosophy, moral principles and theological things, and so on, could not properly be meaningfully discussed in words , they could nevertheless somehow be expressed or shown. This distinction between "saying" and "showing" was difficult for many people to understand and some who did understand it simply rejected it. Critics in this latter camp included John L. Austin and Gilbert Ryle, who were known as ordinary language philosophers. Austin in his disdain for Wittgenstein and his work went so far as to call him a charlatan.[8] Philosophers of language on the whole though, nevertheless proceeded on down the same course, being skeptical about moral and religious discourse in general, and holding that theses realms of discourse proceeded generally from a misunderstanding of the logical nature of language, especially as that relates to the functions of general nouns, in that they treated general nouns in the same way as the names for particular things.[9]

But caught up as they were in these debates, many of the language philosophers managed to overlook some very important and potentially helpful themes in the *logic of language*. Wittgenstein himself later came to a very different conclusion, namely

[7] See A. J. Ayer's work in general here and in particular his *Language, Truth, and Logic*.

[8] Viewing Wittgenstein as a charlatan or worse is perhaps understandable when we remember the pretentious manner with which he presented his *Tractatus* to a publisher when he him that the work was in two parts, the first being the manuscript that he had sent him and the second being the one he didn't send him, the unspoken bit.

[9] Austin and Ryle for their part came to be described as *ordinary language* philosophers, since they regarded ordinary language as embodying reliable views on all sorts of topics, even in the complex discussions of chemists or physicists.

that the *purposes* of the speaker or writer are perhaps the greatest clue to the meaning of their discourse. He also identified a considerable number of purposes that had to be kept in mind while interpreting language. A speaker might be making a joke, issuing a command, expressing pain (ouch!), using an analogy, and so on. So language can be viewed as a game or puzzle of sorts when trying to understand what a speaker means by bearing in mind their purpose. This insight can be captured, extended, and illustrated by the following diagram, where a *language game* is applied to something or other with a view to achieving a *purpose* or purposes.

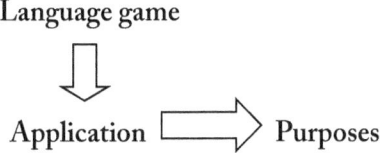

This notion it seems can be successfully applied to all sorts of enterprises. Mathematical science for instance can be seen to boil down to finding the mathematical game that will best fit the purposes of the study. The Danish physicist Neils Borg had the idea that the structure of an atom was like the planets moving round the sun, with electrons whizzing round the nucleus in various orbits. Unfortunately he could only make his mathematics fit this notion in the first shell (hydrogen and helium). But the young German mathematician, Werner Heisenberg, was able to make the mathematics work for all shells (orbits) by dividing the quantum of energy in each electron in two. Borg objected that this was impossible since each electron is defined as a quantum of energy which was fixed and indivisible. If you tried to add energy to it, it did not become more energetic but only moved up to the next orbit: and if you subtracted energy it moved down one shell. The two of them went at it for a year or two and by modifying the various mathematical games finally got them to fit the theory while keeping the quantum of energy intact. Einstein went through a similar series of trials or transformations before he could get his mathematical games to go along with his special theory of relativity.

A Move to Horizontal Logic and Reasoning

The point of the foregoing discussion though, is not to get caught up in trying to understand or arbitrate all the scientific logic and reasoning. Instead, we need to look at the general view of logic represented by game theory, and it is a radical move away from the logic of the syllogism associated with Aristotle with which we began, where you start with a true statement and from there try to logically deduce the consequences from it.

The syllogism then can aptly be described as *vertical logic,* where you proceed from the true statement at the top and try to argue downward to the conclusion you are trying to prove at the bottom. The linguistic model that we have described has rather a different form. It embodies a *horizontal logic.* Here comparison takes place between competing proposals (or games) set side by side to see which one fits best.

The vertical approach produces uncertainty since our attention is focused on flaws and imperfections and so doubts are cast on the entire case being made. The horizontal method, on the other hand, does not get bogged down by minor flaws because it surveys and identifies the best option from those on offer.

The precise game that horizontal reasoning pursues is the one that suits the matter for consideration. So just as mathematicians will appropriately employ the symbols from their field in their studies, chemists might deploy mathematical symbols as well as models with colored balls and matchsticks in their endeavors. Historians often use smaller stories and piece them together to find the most plausible fit to the facts that they are considering. Courtroom lawyers also use what are termed *story logics* to decide whether someone apprehended on the roof of a jewelry store was an electrician or a burglar. Philosophers and theologians do much the same thing in a more general way, seeing which of several views or viewpoints best explains the facts they are considering.

This horizontal approach then, opens up the possibility of meaningful discussion and thoughtful argument about history, moral questions, theology and much more. The horizontal approach therefore, is the method used in the course of this book as we go about the tasks our faiths sets for thinking about God.

SUGGESTIONS FOR FURTHER READING

Ayer, A. J. *Language, Truth, and Logic*. New York: Dover Publications, 1952. Print.

Nidditch, P. H. *The Development of Mathematical Logic*. New York: Free Press of Glencoe, 1962. Print.

David Foster. *The Philosophical Scientists* (New York: 1993)

Bowser, Richard. *Foundations of the Law*. Forthcoming, Spring 2015. This book looks at the application of game theory to jurisprudence using technical terms and symbols.

J. Stanley McQuade *What Wittgenstein Should Have Said*. Article forthcoming in the Campbell Law Review.

Lewis, C S. *Mere Christianity*. New York: Macmillan, 1958. Print.

II

Thinking about the Bible

For Christians the Bible is the Word of God. If we do not believe that the Bible is the preeminent source of our knowledge of God and guide for our thinking and living, we are wandering lost in the desert or adrift on the open sea without compass or chart. This conviction about the scriptures holds for all denominations, Catholic and Orthodox as well as Protestants, Evangelicals, Pentecostals or any other kind of Christian you care to mention. There has been a great revival of interest in the Bible among Churches that had for a time perhaps soft pedaled their dependence on the Bible for doctrine and direction. Pope Benedict XVI, recently retired, wrote many books and always approached any question with a serious discussion of the scriptures, beginning with the Old Testament and from there going on to the Gospels and the rest of the New Testament. I imagine that the same approach holds true for the new Pope too, for there has been a great rediscovery or reemphasis on the Bible among Catholics.

But as Christians we do not all see the Bible as God's Word in the same way. Some see it as virtually dictated by God with every statement in it scientifically true and historically accurate. Others see it differently but still view it as the Word of God, as I think we must. We will consider here three questions.

- What sort of book is the Bible, and how should it be described?
- What do we mean, and what do we not mean, when we say that the Bible is God's Word?
- How should we read the Bible?

In answer to the first question, the Bible is not a book so much as it is a library, a large number of books written at different times and in varying circumstances. And it was not dictated, but written by the various authors as human beings, of flesh and blood.

The characters and personalities, beliefs and perspectives of the writers are still there, and plain to be seen. God did not work around them but through them. But how can we describe the Bible as a whole? Do these numerous books have a theme so that they can be regarded as one book? There are several possible answers to this question, but the best, and the one that Christians have generally held, is that the Bible is the Book of Jesus. The Old Testament prophesies and prepares for His coming, gathering a people to receive and understand Him; the gospels present Him; and the rest of the New Testament deals with His workings in His body, the Church, with the final book, the Apocalypse of St. John, describing the triumph of Christ. The late Bishop Marion Edwards was fond of saying that it is the only book that you should begin to read in the middle, with the Gospels.[1]

We might begin to answer the second question—What we do mean when we say the Bible is God's Word?—by saying what the Bible is not. It is not, despite what many Christians themselves suggest, a book of science. Many well educated and thoughtful Christians try to harmonize biblical views of the world with those of modern science. I respect them but I cannot join them. If God was communicating science to us what science would he use? His people of old would not have known what He was talking about; and even today, it would not only be virtually impossible but nearly unimaginable to describe everything in scientific terms that makes sense now and also accounts for future developments. It is indeed very difficult to reconcile Einstein's science with our ordinary common sense, never mind the Bible. The scientific picture of the universe is currently rather weird from the common sense perspective. What God has given us in the Bible is a simple common sense way of looking at the world and our place in it, viewed from the Divine perspective. And it is supremely adequate for that purpose. The sky may not be a bowl placed over a plate—with the earth floating on water—but simply looking at it as the ancients did, it certainly appears that way. The book of Genesis therefore rightly uses this simple picture to tell us rather central and important things, among them,

---
[1] He was resident Bishop of United Methodist Church in North Carolina from 1996–2004.

that the world did not arrive by accident but was created by God in a marvelous and wonderful way; that this world has a Divine purpose; that we are in it to carry out that purpose; and that while we have failed, God is proceeding to restore us and it.[2] This is the meaning of the story of the Garden of Eden, the tower of Babel and other stories in the early part of the Genesis text, and whatever science comes along with we can still see creation in these terms. The great Swiss theologian, Emil Brunner, has commented that he will not bother to have a serious discussion about life and living with anyone who has not read and reflected on the early chapters of the Book of Genesis. Their views without that grounding, he says, are bound to be superficial.

The same thing holds for history. The Bible contains historical narratives, but their purpose is not to describe exactly what happened in the manner of modern historical scholarship. The so called historical books are describing God's action in the development of God's family, the people of Israel. Indeed in the Jewish Bible, they are not designated as history but as prophesy, which describes them more accurately.

All this is not to say that the Bible history is fiction, anything but. The more we learn about it the more we realize that the people who witnessed the things it describes were there, or had witness accounts to go on, and described them accordingly. The great miracle of the Exodus, where Moses led the Israelites through the sea which divided to let them pass through, sounds ridiculous. But is it even more ridiculous to say that they made up the entire story of the greatest event in their history? It rings true to what we know about God, and detailed study of the event shows several ways in which it might have happened. Moses was directed by God to change direction away from the natural route round the north end of the Gulf of Aqaba and take the Israelites into a narrow valley further south, leading to the sea. Here they were trapped, with Pharaoh's famous chariots, the Panzer tanks of the age, in hot pursuit. The Gulf of Aqaba is very deep elsewhere but at this point its floor had been built up by silt from rivers running into it so that it was relatively shallow. The Book

---

[2] The story of salvation really begins with Abraham but glimpses of it can be seen in the earlier stories.

of Exodus describes how the miracle happened. A cold East wind blew all night long and this, funneled through a narrow gorge, drove the shallow water up on either side and froze it in position.[3] The Israelites crossed over safely, but when he sun rose and the Egyptians tried to cross over behind them the ice melted and they were washed away.[4] This is still a great miracle, for God is in control, and He works the switches and pushes the buttons as He chooses. Miracles are only mysterious to us, not to God. This need not even be exactly what happened on that great occasion, but this shows why we should be slow to write off the Old Testament miracles, or likewise the New Testament miracles, as imaginative fiction. Those who described them were there, or in touch with those who were there, and we were not. But to return to the main theme here, the Bible histories were not given to tell us exactly what happened but to describe God's workings in history. And as such they are interesting, illuminating and helpful, providing guidance for us today. And the other Books of the Old Testament are likewise wonderful. The Psalms of David (and Moses, the sons of Korah, and all the others) represent the deepest feelings of the writers and do so very honestly. When they couldn't understand why God was not helping them they said so. And they speak to our deepest feelings and concerns today.

When we turn to the rest of the Old Testament, the prophets (*naviim*), the Book of Job and the other writings (*kethuvim*, as the Hebrew scholars called them), all speak to us of God, and the more we read them the closer we feel drawn to God and so we correctly consider them as containing the wisdom of God.

When we turn to the New Testament we are drawn closer still to God by the accounts of those who saw and walked with the Lord. We can recall as Jesus said to Phillip, "he that has seen me has seen the Father". The Acts of the Apostles is perhaps the most inaccurately described of all books for it tells us little or nothing

---

[3] This mechanism has been demonstrated using electric fans to simulate the strong wind.

[4] Chariot wheels have been described and photographed in the sand here, although the authenticity of these photographs have been, like everything else, disputed.

about most of the apostles.[5] Luke, the author, clearly considered it as a description of the things that Jesus *continued* to do. For it is the story of the formation and workings of the Body of Christ, His Church, through which He is still present and active on earth. The New Testament Epistles likewise tell us of the story of that body, not in idealized terms but by presenting the members of the Body as they were, as fallible human beings. Yet to them and through them God revealed His Truth. The Apocalypse of John, that strangest of books, is nevertheless the cap on the Bible, for it speaks of the triumph of Christ and does so in inspiring terms.[6] The writer indeed, can only burst into hymns and songs at times as the wonderful narrative proceeds. Many of these have been put to music for us, for example by George Frederick Handel in his oratorio *The Messiah*.

The final question for us to address here, is how should we read the Bible? This is no simple matter for the beginner, and there is just no easy way to get into the Bible other than by reading it. Thankfully, some useful hints have been provided by those who have studied it before us.

First, it is perhaps best to start with the gospels, to begin in the middle as Bishop Edwards put it, and from there go on to explore the rest of the Bible.

Second, after beginning in this manner, we can then use the gospels as the key in interpreting the rest of the Bible, and it no doubt needs interpreting. In this way we employ what's called *progressive revelation,* where the earlier must be understood in the light of the later, because, after all, the full message is only displayed when Jesus arrives. And the same is true of the New Testament. The disciples were often slow to learn the implications of Christ's teachings and St. Paul and the writers of the other epistles had to wrestle with problems of one kind or another, for instance, what to make of the laws of Moses in the light of what Christ had said. And much the same could be said about other

---

[5] The first chapter of Acts describes the Gospel as the "former treatise" and says that it is about what Jesus *began* to do. Acts then would be what God *continued* to do.

[6] The great John Calvin wrote a commentary on every book in the Bible except the Apocalypse, which he simply couldn't fathom.

problems that emerged in the early days of the church which can be found in the letters of the apostles. The apostle Peter remarked in his second letter, that Paul had expressed many ideas (about how to apply the Christian gospel to new situations) and commented that these are difficult to understand and that foolish persons have misinterpreted them to their harm. But though much even of the New Testament is difficult to interpret, if we view the sayings of Paul and the other disciples in the light of the teachings and actions of Jesus we will not go far astray.

Third, we need to remember that we don't have to struggle with every book and every part of the Bible all at once. We can focus on the books and parts that we can understand and which are helpful to us. Someone locking at the uneven wear of the Bible of an older Christian said "there are waters here that you haven't fished." The old disciple answered wisely, "I fish where I know I can catch something".

A fourth thing to say here is to listen as we read, to actively listen for God's word for us now. There is no part of the Bible where something will not just hit you; where some word will act to inspire and help you and this can be God's Word for you for that day, and we should therefore be attentive to this.

The last thing to note here is that I have written this chapter with the hope of encouraging Christians to get the Bible off the shelf so that they read it and trust it and learn to love it. It is after all God's Word, and His Word to us, and we should therefore read it constantly, eagerly and expectantly. If we do this we will almost inevitably fall in love with the Bible and it will make us wise unto salvation. My wife and I have noted how our Christian parents, not notable for their formal education, nevertheless had a wise word for almost every situation and particularly for when troubled times called. And those wise words came from the Bible, and most often were the words of Jesus Himself.

With all this in hand then it will prove worthwhile if we dig in further on some topics related to our beloved Bible, so I'll turn to some of these in what follows of this chapter.

The Canon of Scripture

The canon of scripture refers to those books which are recognized by the Church as properly belonging in the Bible. Of course, the books themselves were preserved and circulated long before they were listed as canonical.

The Old Testament scriptures were recognized in several stages.

- The five books of the law (*torah*) are otherwise known as the Pentateuch meaning five scrolls. We first hear of them when the scribe Ezra read them to the people in the year BC 397 (Neh 8:1). They were around of course, though perhaps neglected, long before then.
- The prophets (*naviim*) represent a larger group of texts. The term prophesy was of course applied to the writings of those we would consider prophets, Isaiah, Jeremiah, Ezekiel, and the twelve minor prophets, but it is also used to refer to books that we might consider historical, such as Joshua, Judges, Samuel, and Kings since God's will was being made known in them to Israel
- The writings (*kethuvim*) include all the rest of the books of the Old Testament, such as Psalms, Proverbs, Job, Ruth, Ecclesiastes, Lamentations, Esther, Daniel (which we might consider prophetic), Nehemiah and Chronicles.

This represents the Hebrew canon recognized by the Masoretic scholars who, from the time of Ezra onward, devoted themselves to preserving and copying the Jewish scriptures. But there was also the Greek canon, based on the Septuagint (or LXX, both terms meaning "seventy"), the Greek version of the Jewish bible, prepared by some seventy scholars in Egypt. Legend has it that King Ptolemy wished to provide the scriptures for Israelites in Egypt who no longer spoke Hebrew but only *koine*, or common Greek. He is said to have gathered 72 elders and placed each of them in a separate room, and instructing each of them to translate the Torah into Greek. Miraculously they all came up with the same translation, what then became the LXX. And the LXX has additional books not recognized in the Masoretic canon. These additional books are known as the Old Testament Apocrypha.

They include such books as 1 Esdras, 1–4 Maccabees, the book of Baruch, the book of Judith, 2 Esdras, Sirach (Ecclesiasticus), and Tobit etc.

The LXX canon is recognized by both the Roman and Orthodox churches and quotations from the Apocrypha are given here and there by St. Paul and other New Testament writers. However, as we noted above, these additional books were rejected by the Masoretic scribes. The apocryphal Old Testament books were also rejected by Luther and the protestant reformers generally, and largely on doctrinal grounds, since they allow prayers for the dead and some other items that were difficult to swallow. The reformers did, however, allow that they might be read with profit.[7]

The New Testament writings were in circulation but not collected and treated as a unit until perhaps the latter part of the second century. We know for instance that Ignatius, Bishop of Antioch, who wrote letters to various churches as he was taken to Rome to be martyred in the early second century, had a box containing the letters of St. Paul. More or less comprehensive collections were made later in the second century and the canon of New Testament writings was for all intents and purposes officially recognized at the Council of Nicea in AD 325. Numerous additional writings, especially gospels, while written allegedly by apostles were rejected by the Church, indicating that other considerations, such as doctrinal and pastoral factors, played a part in determining what made the cut. Much has been made of these gospels, in particular that they represent a genuine Christian tradition which was suppressed, but they seem largely to have been Gnostic works attributed to the apostolic writers to give them credibility.[8] It has been suggested that the Emperor Constantine railroaded this selection process at Nicea for political ends, but it is much more likely that the main body of orthodox Christians

---

[7] The 39 Articles of the Church of England take this same position on the Old Testament Apocrypha.

[8] The much touted Gospel of Thomas is clearly a Gnostic work, though it may contain a saying of Jesus here and there. Gnostics had a preoccupation with secret knowledge (*gnosis*) which some had to the exclusion of others, and clearly this wouldn't sit well with a Gospel that was meant to be heard and preached to all.

rejected many of the candidates for inclusion on the grounds mentioned above.

The Preservation of the Bible text

The Old Testament text was finalized by the fourth century AD by groups of Jewish Scholars known as the Masoretes. These folk operated in several centers in Israel and also in Babylon. The Ben Asher family of Masoretes have tended to be viewed as the most important and their text has been generally preferred. In addition to finalizing the text the Masoretes also standardized the pronunciation of the Hebrew words and provided symbols representing vowels known as pointing (the original Hebrew texts only supplied a few vowels and the rest was left to the imagination and ingenuity of the reader).[9] As was mentioned earlier, in the second century BC the Hebrew text had been translated into what is known as the Spetuagint, or LXX. And since the LXX predates the Masoretic text this allows scholars to check up on the work of the Masoretes. The Old Testament passages found among the Dead Sea scrolls have also been used to the same effect and the Masoretic text has proved by and large to be reliable.

With the New Testament text the story is somewhat different. The major extent Greek manuscripts date back to no earlier than the fourth century, though these can be checked in part by earlier translations into various languages and again they have proved to be largely reliable. The New Testament was early on translated into a number of languages but especially into common Latin, then widely used in the Roman Empire. Old **Latin** translations were superseded by the vulgate (common Latin) version of St. Jerome in the late fourth century which soon gained wide recognition. By the thirtieth century the **Vulgate** had more or less replaced the old Latin bibles. The revival of learning in the thirteenth century affected theological as well as secular studies and there was a great deal of interest in producing Bibles and formatting them for study and other uses. Paris was a great center for this kind of enterprise and Bibles were not only copied

---

[9] The Masoretes are said to have destroyed all other versions after they had finalized the text of the Hebrew Bible.

there but divided up into chapter and verse very much as they are at present. This enabled scholars to cite a particular chapter and verse in their work more easily and to a common standard. Tables listing the various chapters and an introduction to each book were other features of these works. The **Paris Bibles** indeed, were generally structured much as Bibles are at present except that the order of the books, in both Old and New Testament, could vary quite a lot.

By the sixteenth century the Vulgate had become the official version of the Roman Catholic Church and versions in local languages were beginning to appear. Often these were associated with movements that were critical of the Catholic Church such as the Waldensians and Cathars. Such books were prohibited in various places and copies burned where found, but eventually translations into various languages became common and widely accepted.

In 1966 **The Jerusalem Bible** was published in response to a papal encyclical of Pope Pius XII which encouraged translations directly from the original manuscripts instead of from the Vulgate. The work was carried out by Dominican scholars in Jerusalem, hence the name. It was originally produced in French, and the English versions were at least initially translations from the French, with referral for checkup purposes to the original languages. It has been widely accepted as reliable and scholarly work.

The **King James Bible** produced in the sixteenth century continues to be revered, especially since many passages from it had been learned off by heart in Sunday school and other places. But the language, though hallowed by time and association, is archaic and it was also produced before the great fourth century manuscripts of the New Testament had been rediscovered and published, Numerous modern English variations and versions have been produced to replace it as a result.

The **New English Bible** was a massive undertaking involving concern about the English language used as well as the accuracy of the translation from the Biblical originals. The New Testament was published first and the entire Bible made available in 1970.

The **New International Version** (NIV) was produced by Evangelical Scholars in the United States and has proved very popular. An updated version in 2001 proved somewhat controversial due to the adoption of gender neutral language here and there, so that the original is still preferred by many readers. The NIV has been considered by many to be the successor to the Authorized Version

However, gains in intelligibility from these new translations were often offset with loss of familiarity and reduced ability on the part of many persons to learn and quote from the Bible. The **New King James** version was produced to remedy this situation, retaining as much of the old phrasing as possible and only making changes where really needed, for example in those places where the original manuscripts used to produce the King James Bible were deemed inaccurate, and readings from the more recently discovered great codices were now preferred.

Allowing Catholic lay persons to read the Bible for themselves continued to be viewed into modern times as somehow dangerous and to be discouraged. But since Vatican II, Catholics generally have been encouraged to read the Bible; and Protestant and Catholic Christians, both lay and clerical, have been better able to converse in a common theological language with fairly accepted criteria for what constitutes Christian doctrine and what does not.

Biblical Interpretation through the Ages

Philo Judeus, the first century BC Jewish philosopher from Alexandria, in attempting to harmonize Hebrew thinking with Greek philosophy, adopted the allegorical method of interpretation for the Old Testament. This made any kind of harmonization of differing viewpoints possible and it was very popular with the Alexandrian church fathers, Clement and Origen. It was used in particular to explain the differences between the Old and New Testaments and can even be found in New Testament writings themselves, such as in the Epistle to the Hebrews. This kind of Biblical exegesis has persisted into modern times especially with less formally educated preachers who often extract moral and spiritual messages from quite ordinary narrative statements, so

Jacob being ordered to arise and go back to Bethel and dwell there becomes a message to backsliders (Gen 35:1). But quite early the allegorical method had its critics who sought to take the text more seriously rather than unearthing hidden allegorical or moral meanings. The emphasis here was on the intent of the authors. St. Thomas Aquinas accepted that there could be spiritual meanings as well as the literal sense of the text, but held that the spiritual sense arose out of the literal sense and should be governed by it.

The reformers, Luther and Calvin were likewise opposed to the allegorical interpretations of scripture and similarly insisted on the intent of the author. But they also added the notion that there was a plain meaning to scripture such that ordinary unlearned persons could understand it and believe and be saved. This plain meaning, they held, should be used to understand difficult or obscure texts.

John Wesley dwelt at some great length on the question and details of the interpretation of Scripture, and in general he followed the lead of Luther and Calvin. But with this difference, he believed that one could only understand the Bible if one was willing to put what they learned from it into effect

Allegorical interpretation as an interpretive method is one that assumes that the Bible has various levels of meaning and tends to focus on the spiritual sense, the moral (or tropological) sense, and the anagogical (or mystical) sense beyond just the literal sense. This classificatory statement was sometimes referred to as the Quadriga, a reference to the Roman chariot drawn by four horses.

The use of allegorical interpretation in the Middle Ages began as a Christian method for studying the differences between the Old Testament and the New (tropological or figurative interpretation). Christian scholars believed both the Old and New Testament were equally inspired by God and sought to understand the differences between Old Testament and New Testament Laws. Medieval Scholars believed that the Old Testament functions as an allegory of New Testament events, so for example, Jonah and the Whale naturally bring Jesus' death and resurrection to mind. According to the Old Testament, the prophet Jonah spent three days in the belly of a great fish. Medieval Scholars treated this as an allegory or as something that prefigured Jesus' death and being in the tomb for three days before he rose (see Matt 12:40).

The Bible and Evolution

Darwin's *Origin of Species* challenged Christian belief at two levels. First, it questioned the Genesis account of the creation of the animal world, including humans. This is no great threat unless we think that God intended the Bible to instruct us in science. But Darwinian evolution can be taken to provide an alternative theory of animal creation which does not require divine purpose. It proposes a series of random genetic mutations with the environment weeding out the unsuitable ones and the favorable ones surviving and continuing their line into the future. This more or less mechanical proceeding is definitely adverse to biblical doctrine and has produced an apologetic response from theologians and also from scientists who have a Christian perspective on things. It has been common, in particular, for these critics of evolutionary explanations to point out gaps between the appearance of one species and the next and to insist that something more than random variations and natural selection is required to explain these transitions. These gaps though have been at least partially filled by discoveries of intermediate species or their remains which seems to suggest that the missing links will eventually all be found and the Darwinian hypothesis validated with no need for divine intervention. This focus on the "God of the Gaps" then, has not proved a helpful ploy for Christian apologists and indeed misses the real problem for mechanical versions of evolution, namely, the difficulty of explaining how simple life forms or even inanimate matter can develop into extraordinarily complex beings. It beggars imagination how a lifeless lump of matter could appear and then develop into and produce even the simplest of the creatures that we know. The mechanisms and systems required are so incredibly complex, both in themselves and in their relationship to the environment, that random genetic variation and weeding out by the environment seem to be hopelessly crude explanatory tools, like using a can opener to open a safe. The success of scientific explanations then, does not argue against design but for it. As one wondrous finding succeeds another an accidental or random process seems less and less believable if we apply here our horizontal method of reasoning to this matter. On the contrary the complexity and sophistication of the findings makes it less and less likely that they were the result of pure chance and therefore we conclude that God's hand of providence is the guiding principle in creation.

SUGGESTIONS FOR FURTHER READING

Keller, Werner. *The Bible as History.* New York: Bantam, 1982. Print.

Drummond, Henry. "The Ascent of Man." *The Henry Drummond Reader.* Radford, VA: Wilder Publications, 2008. Print. This classic piece is republished here and still well worth reading.

Fee, Gordon D., and Douglas K. Stuart. *How to Read the Bible for All Its Worth.* Grand Rapids, Mich.: Zondervan, 2003. Print.

Duguid, Iain M. *Is Jesus in the Old Testament?* P & R, 2013. Print.

Morgan, Robert, and John Barton. *Biblical Interpretation.* Oxford: Oxford University Press, 1988. Print.

III

Thinking about God

Learning my Sunday School Catechism as a child I imbibed the following questions and answers:
> Q. What is God? A. God is a spirit, One that always was and always will be.
> Q. Where is God? A. God is everywhere.
> Q. Who is God? A. God is our Father in Heaven.

Somewhere else in the catechism (or just somewhere else) I learned that God is infinite in power, wisdom and goodness.

When we start thinking about these statements the first problem we encounter is the notion of infinity. God always was there and always will be there (infinite time). God is everywhere (infinite space). And then there's infinite power, wisdom and love. The notion of infinity of any kind boggles the mind. We can represent it with a special mathematical symbol or a special word or picture, but we cannot imagine it or comprehend it in any completely satisfying way. Modern mathematical physicians, and some very imaginative theologians, say odd things about space and time such as that time and space were not always there but somehow arrived and appeared at some point in the story. This kind of language is fine for their particular purposes, but to the ordinary mind there must be infinity of time and space even though we cannot imagine them: we are just stuck with them.[1] I once had a discussion with a friend in school about space. He said it was finite, it had to stop somewhere. I objected that if you took a space ship to the edge of space and stuck your hand out of

---

[1] Language philosophers may view the problems here as being due to mixing two irreconcilable languages; the language of common sense, where space and time go on forever, with the language of astrophysics, where they do not. But most of us live most of the time in the world of common sense where the problem remains.

the window it had to go somewhere. He responded that I couldn't get my hand out of the window because there was nowhere for it to go. I was stymied, but still think I had the better argument. We can't imagine infinity but it is there nevertheless.

Applying these considerations to our understanding of God, the same is true. We cannot imagine infinite power, or infinite presence, or infinite goodness but we are stuck with them. Once we accept that an accidental universe is an infinitely low probability option, we are left with the task of saying something positive about the designer, a Supreme Being who is infinitely powerful etc. beyond our imagining,

Who is this God? Physicists and philosophers who cannot accept the idea of an accidental universe, may nevertheless qualify their opinion by saying that when they speak of an intelligent designer they are not talking about God as represented in the Bible. But if not, what are they talking about? If there is a being that made everything, then that Being also made mankind. Would or could an impersonal Being (like the great insect for instance described in some science fiction novels) place at the apex of creation beings totally unlike their Creator. The notion that God is a person who made us in His image (though to a much lesser degree) is much more believable: in fact the reverse is hardly persuasive. We are persons, we have feelings, and moral and aesthetic feelings at that, and it is hard to credit that our Creator is anything less.

We have talked thus far about knowing God from Nature, but there is a limit to this knowledge. Nature reveals infinite power, and infinite creative wisdom, but what about the love and caring and all the personal attributes of God that we read about in the Bible. St. Paul in the first chapter of his letter to the Romans says that "since the creation of the world, God's invisible qualities, His eternal power and Divine Nature, have been clearly seen in the things that He has made" (Rom 1:20), and this is true as far as it goes. But it does not go far enough. There is also the voice of Revelation telling us more about God. The writer to the Hebrews sums this up when he says that "God in these last days has spoken to us by His Son." (Heb 1:2). Nature itself can be a tricky thing to read. It is a dangerous place with the continents floating on molten rock which from time to time erupts in volcanoes and earthquakes and huge tidal waves that sweep away everything in their path. No doubt there are messages in these things; that life is not meant to be a picnic, that it is a serious business, and that there are winners and losers. But there are also, be it noted, some hints of our caring Father even in nature, red in tooth and claw. The caring family is found in elephants and lions and other communal animals. Prey animals in the food chain are eaten by predators, but this is good in the sense that it ensures health and vitality in the system as a whole.[2] So death and danger, and families that care for one another are all here intertwined. Partners care for one another too, and mothers, and sometimes fathers, may sacrifice their very lives for their young. Mother rabbits will attack a stoat in defense of their young; boars will turn and chase leopards, their natural enemies, to protect the young piglets; deer too will take similar risks on occasion. Of additional interest, it seems that when a prey animal is caught it goes into a sort of anesthetic state where it feels no pain. A surgeon in Vermont, a Dr. Clap by name, developed and tested surgical techniques for operating on sheep (and he had a special license to do so). He had used spinal anesthesia on the animals but found that they showed no signs of pain when they were simply held fast. He duplicated these results hundreds of times, which all goes to suggest that there's a little bit of extra kindness built into the system.

Following out the suggestion we see in Hebrews, we find that in the Bible we are given more than just a hint about our God's character. We have a message from God Himself, which reveals to us his inner nature. We have in the Bible a drawing aside of the curtain to show the deeper and more personal character of the Creator and all He has done for us. So that when we say with the catechism "God is our Father in heaven," we know much more what that means than nature alone can reveal, so that when we pray we can also truly believe it when we call God "Our Father."

There is much more to be said about God. He has revealed Himself to us most fully in His son Jesus, the Word made flesh, and this is the topic to be considered in the next chapter. Before

---

[2] When the top predators disappear the prey animals well-being becomes endangered.

turning our attention fully to that topic though we'll first look more closely at the biblical notion of God in God's self.

The Doctrine of the Trinity

In orthodox terminology, God is described as "Father, Son and Holy Spirit; three persons, one God". This precise formula is not found anywhere in the Bible, but the materials from which it is constructed are clearly present. God the Father is named in both Testaments; the Divine qualifications of the Son are prominent in the New Testament; and the Holy Spirit is described in personal terms. In the fourth gospel in particular, the Holy Spirit is depicted as a person quite distinct from the Father and the Son. Consequently the doctrine of the Trinity has, for most of the Christian era, been considered a major pillar of the orthodox faith.[3]

The problems associated with the Trinitarian formula have been first, distinguishing it from polytheism (in this case tritheism) and on the other hand expressing the unity of the Godhead as we find it say in the Law of Moses.[4] Arius, a presbyter of Alexandria in the fourth century, avoided the problem by making the Son a creature though a very exalted one ("there was a time when he was not"). Origen had earlier sought to clarify aspects of the Trinity by using a new term, saying that the Son was not created but *eternally generated* from the Father, and the same could of course be said of the Spirit, meaning that there was never a time when they were not.[5]

This terminological solution seems a little artificial and insufficient on its own. We would prefer, as Trinitarians, to express the unity of the Godhead more explicitly. The orthodox church fathers used the term *persona* (three Persons one God) to describe how there could be distinct persons in the single Godhead. A

---

[3] Baptists who tend to be averse to creeds nevertheless accept certain creedal formulations as central and axiomatic. Recently a Baptist writer described himself as a Baptist, an Evangelical and a Trinitarian.

[4] "Hear O Israel the Lord thy God the Lord is one, and thou shallot love the Lorde thy god etc. (Deut. 6:4)..

[5] Origen was a prominent theologian of the Alexandrian school in the third century.

persona was originally used to describe a part played by an actor in a play. This was hardly what the Church fathers meant, they were rather using this term to express the idea of separate personalities within the single unity of the Godhead. But again the achievement seems to be rather terminological than real.

In modern times, with a greater appreciation of the nature of personality and even the recognition that one person can have several personalities, the idea of separate personalities or personae within one person can be more readily be appreciated as a reality rather than being just a matter of fancy terminology. And while it is true that having multiple personalities is generally considered to be a medical disorder rather than a normal state of affairs, there is perhaps here some conceptual help in the notion of three persons in one being.

As a further comment it has been argued that the Trinitarian formula expresses the idea that God in Himself, in His very nature, is essentially social which, taken to the ultimate degree, can be seen to express the idea that God is love. Along these lines it can also be said that there is no suggestion of any possible disharmony among the three persons. St. Paul (in 1 Cor 15:28) speaks of the consummation of all things when "the Son will place Himself under God, and God will rule completely over all." This is commonly termed "subordination," but it must be seen in the context of the Fourth Gospel where the agreement between Father and Son is absolute, and in light of what Jesus himself says, that "I and the Father are one" (John 10:30).

In attempting to explain the Trinity we must remember that we are clearly taking language to and, at times, even beyond its farthest limits when we try to describe the inner nature of God. In short it is one of those areas where we are stretched theologically and at times need to be content to make do with metaphors and illustrations, (like the analogy with the shamrock, attributed to St. Patrick). And in light of all this the classical formula of "three persons, one God" is perhaps as good as any.

SUGGESTIONS FOR FURTHER READING

The article "Trinity" on Wikipedia is well worth reading, as is "St. Patrick: The Trinity and the Shamrock," also to be found on Wikipedia.

González, Justo L. *A History of Christian Thought*. Abingdon, 2014. Print.

Beet, Joseph Agar. *Through Christ to God: a Study in Scientific Theology*. New York: Hunt & Eaton, 1893. Print. Part 4 which discusses the New Testament basis for the Trinity is particularly helpful.

Feldmeier, Reinhard, and Hermann Spieckermann. *God of the Living: A Biblical Theology*. Waco: Texas, Baylor University Press, 2011. Print.

IV

Thinking about Jesus the Christ

What do we mean when we recite the Apostle's creed and say that we believe in "Jesus Christ His only Son our Lord"? Belief in Jesus as the Son of God is treated as the central point of Christian doctrine, both in the New Testament and in the thinking of the Church ever since. The belief itself grew out of that crucial moment in the training of the disciples when Jesus took them apart to a quiet place and began by asking them "who do the people say that I am?" (Matt 16:13–20) They answered that some say this and some say that. Jesus then went on to ask them the all-important question "who do *you* say that I am?" Peter replied "You are the Christ the Son of the Living God". Jesus then said that this response was not just an opinion that Peter had arrived at by himself, nor heard from somebody else, but it had been revealed to him by God, our Father in heaven. This formula, "Jesus is the Christ the Son of God" was used in the early church to distinguish genuine travelling teachers from itinerant heretics who sponged on and misled the unsuspecting church members. And it has been the typical descriptive title of Jesus ever since and also is central in creedal formulas of the Christian Church.

In his book entitled *Jesus of Nazareth*, Pope Benedict XVI presents a sort of running commentary of his friend Rabbi Jacob Neusner's reflections on Jesus' Sermon on the Mount. The Rabbi is most sympathetic to the teaching of Jesus on the law. It is his final comment, though, that is perhaps the most interesting. He believes that Jesus could only criticize and reformulate the law of Moses as He did, by assuming a divine character and authority, for only God can change the law given to Moses. No human being had the right to reinterpret it as radically as Jesus did, first reciting the law and then saying, "but I say unto you..." This is something that Rabbi Neusner could not accept, and so he rejects the claim that Jesus is divine and instead takes his stand with "the eternal Israel". The Rabbi, as Pope Benedict reads the situation, has hit the nail on the head by identifying the central issue at the heart of the Christian faith: whether Jesus claimed to be the Son of God and whether we can accept this claim ourselves.

The position of the Christian Church is that the New Testament presents Jesus as being the Son of God and that this is also the teaching of Jesus himself. Denying this seems to imply that Jesus was either mistaken (or mad) or was misrepresented by his followers. To decide the truth or falsehood of the Church's claim we need to lay out the choices in the horizontal manner we have adopted in this study. We therefore need to look at the account of Jesus and his teaching as we find it in the Gospels, compare it with the other possible notions about him, and ask which is the most likely to be the truth. In short we are asking if the Gospel account represents what Jesus Himself taught. If it is not then, again in simple terms, it is either an error (or even a delusion) on the part of Jesus himself, or a rewriting of His teaching by the apostles or later disciples in the post-apostolic age. None of these alternatives fits well. The Jesus of the Gospels breathes sanity and it is surely beyond the wit of his disciples, early or later, to fabricate such a person or invent such teaching. In summary then, this central doctrine of the faith must stand or fall on how we see this person and his teaching as described for us in the Gospels.

First up, it must be noted, that the attitude with which we approach the gospels is important. If we are firmly secular in our opinions, unsympathetic to anything not obviously within our experience, and skeptical about anything theological or miraculous, we will not be inclined easily to credit the gospel story as being true. But from a perspective that is sympathetic to the God we've discussed thus far in this book, the incarnation is very much in line with what one would think would happen and in keeping with the character of the God of our faith. The coming of God to earth in person is still admittedly far from our ordinary experience of things, but from a theological perspective it is only what we would expect. The Bible describes God in personal terms and also that we are created as persons, in his image and likeness. Human beings, the pinnacle of creation, were given free will so that they could be partners and companions of God, and not just machines. These qualities and abilities also brought about the possibility that they could stray and even lose sight of their Creator. God, long suffering this state of affairs, repeatedly attempted to bring humanity back to Him. He sent prophets, and He worked in the hearts and minds of people through His Spirit. But what better way could He have acted than to come to His children in person? It is simply appropriate given what we know about God and man. No doubt this is a very bold and up front claim to make, and for our part we are not asked to take just anyone's word for it. We have been provided with the gospel accounts of Jesus so that we can decide for ourselves, as Peter did, whether His claim is credible or not. And this too is exactly what we would expect God to do and indeed what we might want and hope for, that no one decides this for us but ourselves.

Second, it seems to me that if Jesus was just a prophet and teacher, it would be very difficult for his followers, either accidentally or deliberately, to doctor the record in support of a claim for His Divinity. The Gospels do not sound like a work of fiction and attempts to get behind the record and discern the true Jesus as an ordinary man (the Jesus of history) have become even harder to believe than the orthodox view. Fictional heroes are very difficult to draw. We are perhaps more convincing when we depict villains.

Third, the picture of Jesus has been painted by different hands in the Gospels, of which we recognize four as canonical. And they offer very different viewpoints. Matthew represents the Jewish-Christian community in Jerusalem. Mark is traditionally represented as the secretary of Peter and many items in his gospel support the view that one of its sources is this apostle. It characteristically spells out Peter's failures whereas we would expect an apocryphal gospel to focus more on his triumphs. Luke, the good physician and companion of Paul, represents the tradition of St. Paul. Luke's account has been described as the gospel of the gentiles and of women. He was a Greek-style historian (he liked reporting speeches) who had opportunities to meet and mingle with the living apostles and others in Jerusalem to find out what had happened there. The fourth Gospel, notably different in style, draws us still closer to Christ with its timeless witness to Him, and I will discuss this below in some greater depth. We have then, four connected but distinct pictures of Jesus which, despite their differences, unite in their picture of Christ and this is something that would be very difficult to arrange were it not true.

In short, there is every good reason to believe in Jesus as the Christ. But just what are we saying about Him by affirming this? The fourth Gospel says that the Word became Flesh and dwelt among us (John 1). We know this as *the incarnation*, but, again, what does this mean? Christian art often depicts the infant Jesus with a glowing halo around his head. The *monophysite* heretics, denied that Christ incarnate contained a human nature and believed instead that there was only a divine nature present in Jesus. But this is not what the New Testament presents and teaches. The incarnation was a true birth of a real baby. And He was truly human in his ministry. He performed miracles not by his own power alone but by the finger of God. God raised Lazarus from the dead in response to Jesus' prayer. He appears to have only realized who he was gradually and particularly during his baptism in the Jordan by John the Baptist. His emotions were human: He wept at Lazarus tomb and cried out on the cross "my God, why have you forsaken me?" It has been remarked, and rightly so, that the incarnation was a greater miracle than the resurrection. It is certainly less imaginable. But the many puzzles about the nature of Christ must be approached, as we have seen with belief in God, by comparing alternative views. Recapping, these are,

- That the New Testament picture of Christ is true.
- That Jesus was mistaken or even deluded.
- Or, that the followers of Jesus distorted the picture of Jesus, substituting a divine Christ for the original great teacher.

Approached in this manner the first, for all its difficulties, appears as a clear winner. The person and teaching of Jesus are so unique that it is hardly credible that he was deluded or mistaken. And rewriting the original story seems beyond the wit and accomplishments of any of his immediate followers, indeed by their own testimony. This is especially the case with the church later than the lifetime of the first disciples, when we consider that they would have had to reconstruct the story in terms of first century Jewish language(s) and with a background which they had largely no longer shared.

One final point is worth mentioning. Belief in Jesus as Lord has its rational side but it is also presented in the New Testament as something miraculous and beyond ordinary expectations and explanations. Jesus told Peter, when he had pronounced the first creedal statement about Him, that "flesh and blood had not revealed this to him but the Father in Heaven." His faith, in its fullness, was ultimately derived from divine illumination, where the facts were organized and seen as a blinding reality. True belief in Jesus has always been represented as miraculous. It has, like everything else, a rational side, but ultimately it is a special gift of the Holy Spirit. Keep this in mind as we delve deeper in our thinking about Jesus Christ His only Son, our Lord.

The Fourth Gospel

As promised, we'll look here more closely at the unique nature and challenges of John's Gospel witness to Christ. Pope Benedict XVI in his book *Jesus of Nazareth* has a most helpful section on the fourth gospel that can provide a good point of departure for us. Benedict begins by exploding Rudolph Bultmann's view that it is a Gnostic work, a ridiculous position especially when we fully compare the fourth Gospel with known and explicitly Gnostic gospels. Pope Benedict goes on to reach several conclusions of his own which are very appealing.

- For a start, he suggests, it is hard to imagine John's gospel to be a work of fiction or even a worked over version of the gospel story. To begin with, it rings very true. Its style and language are somewhat different from the synoptics as we noted, which is understandable in light of its professed aim of describing something quite different; those more intimate conversations of Jesus with his disciples. We read in the synoptics that Jesus spoke to the crowds in parables, but later explained things privately to his disciples. The fourth gospel records these conversations. There are also more limited

examples of this in the synoptic gospels, such as in Matthew 11, which itself very closely resembles the style and language of the fourth Gospel.
- Rabbinical students did not take notes, they remembered. A good student was described as being like a good cistern that didn't lose a single drop. And such a vessel was the beloved disciple, John. He stored up conversations and other details not present in the other gospels.
- It needs be noted that it is a very Jewish gospel, the work of one well versed in Jewish thought and is replete with accurate references to Jerusalem. There is no mention of the destruction of the city in AD 70 by the Romans, which suggests that it contains a good deal of material from before this date.
- Its particular value is the way that the miracles are treated not just as marvels but as *signs*, as ways of teaching profound truths that are difficult to express adequately in words. So each miracle is followed by interpretative discussion.
- The fourth Gospel also contains a number of conversations of Jesus with various individuals (Nicodemus and the woman at the well, for example), and these ring true as genuine conversations, not literary compositions.

There are some difficulties with the text of the fourth Gospel. The story of the women taken in adultery, and the discussion which follows, for one, since it is missing from some early manuscripts. But the story recorded is so entirely in accord with the rest of the Gospel that few would doubt its authenticity. It is probably best explained either as an omission by later copyists from the original text or as an addition inserted by the apostle in a second version of his work. In short the fourth Gospel is a treasure, and Pope Benedict has done the church great service by his discussion of this entire topic.

The Virgin Birth

The doctrine of the virgin birth of our Savior has been a steadfast element of the faith, especially at Christmas time when it features in cards and also in the children's plays and pageants of the Church Christmas programs. It has not been so popular with theologians who note that it is only found in Matthew's and Luke's gospels and not even mentioned in the other gospels nor in the rest of the New Testament. There is also the problem in related claim that Jesus was of the family and lineage of David, the coming great King of Israel foretold by prophesy. For while Joseph was in the Davidic line we are not told the same about Mary, and then Jesus is referred to as the son of Joseph, "as it was supposed" (Luke 3:23) It has also been remarked that a virgin birth was not strictly necessary, since God could have incarnated Christ in human form with two human parents just as easily as with one.

But this is not all that needs to be said on the subject. Matthew was part of the Jerusalem church and their associated tradition surely merits some credibility. Likewise Luke, the travelling companion of St. Paul and a historian of the Greek order, visited Jerusalem and would have had opportunities to visit and talk with the appropriate people there, many of whom would still have been alive.

The doctrine of the virgin birth is also very appropriate when we consider God's use of miracles. They are not just wonderful events, they are also "signs," those special ways of imparting important knowledge. So the great miracle of the exodus was not just meant to get the Israelites out of Egypt but also to teach vitally important truths about God and themselves. The messiahship of Jesus was similarly accompanied by marvelous signs which expressed, as no words could do, who He was and what His coming was meant to be. So when John the Baptist sent his disciples to ask Jesus if he was the one who was coming or did he have to wait for another, Jesus referred them to the miraculous signs that he was performing, where the lame walk, the blind see and the poor have the good news preached to them" (Matt 11:5), all identifying signs of the Messiah. Likewise the raising of Lazarus from the dead was not just a miraculous event but also expressed the great message of Jesus that He was the resurrection and the life so that whoever believed in him should never die (John 11:26).

The virgin birth then, expresses the incarnation of the divine

Logos in a simple yet profound manner. We ourselves stem from two origins, from our father and our mother. Jesus likewise has two origins with the difference that one of them was divine. This notion helps expresses the incarnation in a way that is both simple and profound. The simplest child can understand it, and the most profound thinkers, drowning as they may be amid the waves of some tricky theological arguments, can find here something precise and definite on which to base their thinking.

God, it has been remarked, is a great dramatist. The story of creation can be seen as a great drama with the infinity of space as the backdrop and the long history of the earth and its creatures as the overture. The truth of the virgin birth can be seen as another example of the artistry of God, accompanying the great event of the incarnation with its interpretative drama.

Christology in the Early Church

It is important to note that the Christians in the early post-apostolic age were not, as might be supposed, in closer contact with the apostles, nor more in line with their thinking than we are. At times it was quite the reverse. They did not have the New Testament as we know it to guide them, and to an extent were on their own. They were also in a different world from the apostles, a gentile world where Greek thinking often dominated. And they were trying, as we all must, to come to terms with the culture of their age. We can view them then, not always as the greatest authorities on Christian thinking, closer to the apostles than we are, but rather as post-apostolic Christians struggling with issues and questions that had not impacted in the same way the original Christian community.

A good deal of the post-apostolic church's difficulties sprang from the Greek perspectives of their culture. After AD 70 the Jewish Christian church was dispersed and the Christians, now mainly gentile, were in a totally different world, a gentile world as different from the Jewish one as oil is to water, from that in which the Church had begun and developed. The educated elements in gentile culture in general featured a great appreciation of intellectual pursuits and systems, and a relative indifference to physical things.[1] Many in the Greek culture regarded the body as a prison and as such opposed to the divine aspirations of the human mind. That the divine Christ should be subjected to the limitations of a human body was then something that they found difficult to understand, and it would have seemed to some that Christ could not have had a real human body. One very early expression of this trend was known as *Docetism*, where Christ only seemed to have a human body, which was in fact a *phantom*.[2] Ignatius, Bishop of Antioch in the province of Asia, on his way to Martyrdom in Rome in the early years of the second century, wrote a number of letters, and in one of these he described certain godless men who taught that Christ did not suffer on the cross since he was a phantom.[3] This view was never seriously entertained by the early Church.

Cerinthus, an Egyptian Christian in the late first century, made a similar accommodation with Greek thought, teaching that Christ was a heavenly being who descended on Jesus at his baptism but left him before the crucifixion. Tertullian suggests that John wrote his gospel and especially its prologue in answer to Cerinthus.

However, a good deal of Jewish thinking still remained in the church and one group, known as *Ebionites*, went to the other extreme, holding that Jesus was a man who was adopted by God as His Son. They based this belief on Psalm 2:7 "Thou art my Son this day have I begotten Thee" (cited in Heb 1:5) and also on the account of Jesus' baptism by John where the Spirit descended on Jesus like a dove (Matt 3:16–18). This view assorts ill, however, with the notion of Jesus as the incarnation of the Son that we find in the New Testament more generally and especially with the prologue to the Gospel of St. John.

But Christian thinkers, while convinced that Jesus was the Son of God and divine, also accepted the central Jewish tenet, expressed in the great commandment in Deuteronomy (Deut 6:4) that God is one, and so were anxious to preserve the unity of the Godhead. And all this brings us squarely back to issues that arose

---

[1] The gnostic gospels sellout in many ways to contemporary Hellenistic thought
[2] From the Greek verb meaning "to appear' or "to seem."
[3] In his *Letter to the Christians in Smyrna*.

in and around our discussion of the Trinity. Sabellius (early in the third century) taught that the Father, Son and Holy Spirit were simply modes of appearances of God. Since this view, termed *modalism*, seemed to imply that God was literally in Christ, this view was sometimes described as *patripassionism*, since it was God who suffered on the cross.

The Alexandrine fathers, Clement and Origen (of the late second century), employed the Greek concept of *Logos,* or Word, to explore these matters.[4] This notion is used after all, in the prologue to the Gospel of St. John to describe Christ. They held that the logos was immanent in the world but also fully incarnate in Jesus. Origen, who was a major Christian apologist, opposed the idea that the Logos was a mere emanation of God, and used the word Son as an equivalent expression. He also taught that Christ was not created but eternally generated from the Father. The teachings of the Alexandrine fathers were not universally approved but some of their ideas paved the way for the development of the unity expressed in the creed of Nicaea.

In the early fourth century, Arius, a presbyter in the Church of Alexandria, taught that while Christ was a divine being, greater than the angels, he was nevertheless a created being, important but subordinate to God the Father. Arius thus stated of Christ that "there was a time when he was not". The great council of Nicaea was called to settle this question, but the orthodox fathers had difficulty in pinning down the Arians, who were very skilled at interpreting any proposed formula in a way that was agreeable to their own views. It is reported that Athanasius, and Hosius (Bishop of Cordova and the emperor's secretary, who presided at the council of Nicaea) while conversing with an Arian bishop, found that he could not stomach the idea that Christ was of the same substance (*homoousios*) as the Father, so straightway they introduced this term into the creed of Nicaea. The term substance to them meant category, that is that Jesus was in the same class of being as God, and this view is found in the words of the Nicene creed that Christ is, "true God from true God, begotten not made, being of the same substance as the father, by whom all

---

[4] Philo of Alexandria, a Jewish philosopher (BC 30–AD 50) used logos to express Old Testament concepts in Greek terms.

worlds were made".

Further controversies arose about the relationship of the two natures, divine and human, in Christ. Appolinaris, Bishop of Laodicea in the late fourth century, taught that the divine logos replaced the human mind in Jesus who was then, it seems, a sort of double entity, with a ghost running the machine.

The fathers of the church in Antioch, notably the great preacher St. John Chrysostom (the golden tongued) differed from Appolinaris and taught that Jesus had two natures, divine and human, which although distinct were conjoined and one. This is more or less the position taken in the Creed of Chalcedon and later confirmed in the fifth and sixth general councils held in Constantinople in AD 451 and 689.

Most Christian people today have trouble understanding what all the fuss was about and tend to think that the real problem is that the relationship of the divine and human in Jesus, which we accept, is a mystery which we cannot hope to explain in human terms and which perhaps is better left alone. But there is something more to be said on this subject. The efforts of the early church fathers were not merely heated disputes about words, but a search for a formula which would express their intuitive notions about who Jesus was. The Bible does not open up for us the mystery of the person of Christ, but it does provide us with some guidelines to help our thinking on this important matter. The various statements about Christ in the gospels and the letters of Paul and the other apostolic writers, were used to refute the too easy attempts of the heretics to accommodate Christian thought to ideas current in their culture. Indeed, as we made note of, the virgin birth can be seen as a teaching miracle (a sign as the fourth gospel would have it) representing the divine and human elements in the person of Jesus in a similar way that each parent contributes to the nature of a child, and this conforms to the creed of Chalcedon where the two natures are together not separated but united in one human person.

The Resurrection of Jesus

Like life after death itself, resurrection from the dead is not part of our normal experience. If someone asserted that a person we know had been raised from the dead (and I don't mean resuscitated) our first reaction would be to refuse to believe them. The resurrection of Jesus is somewhat different. For a start he was not an ordinary person but the anointed one (the Christ) who Himself taught that he would be killed and rise again on the third day.

Much has been written considering the evidence for His resurrection and in our horizontal terms the question boils down to whether other explanations for the resurrection tradition are more credible or not. The resurrection tradition is quoted in several places in the New Testament which suggests that it predates the gospels which quote it. It states among other things that the first witnesses were the women and that nobody believed them. Perhaps the best way to approach this question then, is to look at the detailed narratives in the gospels and see if they are credible or not, in the sense that their truth is more credible than alternative hypotheses.

The tomb itself was that of a wealthy Jew carved in a rock. It was important to prevent criminals from ransacking or disturbing such a place so a door was required and this was commonly a large heavy stone. In a tomb prepared in advance like this it would be more in the form of a wheel which was rolled into a groove and which would be very difficult to move out of, so forming a simple and effective seal. "Who rolled back the stone?" is therefore a difficult question, especially if the tomb were guarded. And we would expect the tomb to be guarded, as recorded in the gospels, to prevent the disciples removing the body and claiming that a resurrection had taken place. Additionally, if the disciples removed the body one would have to ask why they did it, since they apparently were surprised by encountering the risen Jesus. But if they did so deliberately, and it would have to be fraudulently, how then did they become so bold and confident travelling all over the world preaching Jesus and the resurrection. And what did they expect to gain from all this except a hard life and a harder death.

The record itself in the gospels is compelling, and it would have been difficult to fabricate. There are also some interesting features about it. For instance the young disciple John looked into the tomb and saw the linen grave clothes lying there, and he believed. What can have been so special about the grave clothes that convinced him? The burial garments of a Palestinian Jew were first of all a long strip of cloth, about three feet wide and twelve feet long, which was folded longitudinally round the body covering back and front. This was held in place by a strip or strips of cloth wound round and round the body like a bandage. There was also a separate face cloth. If Jesus was not dead and had recovered (the swoon theory), these would have either been missing or unwound and indeed scattered. If some persons removed the body, they would either have taken it with the burial clothes in place, the most likely way, or else they would have left them behind in disorder. If the burial clothes were still there but with no body inside them, this would have been remarkable and the young disciple seeing this would then indeed be moved to believe what he had been told and perhaps half believed about Jesus dying and rising again.

The upshot of all this is that alternative versions of the event appear even less plausible than the story of the resurrection as recounted in the New Testament.

The Shroud of Turin

This brings us to one more piece of evidence, and an important one, namely the shroud of Turin. This is a long piece of cloth about three feet in width and twelve feet long which has an image of a naked male, front and back, who has been whipped bloody and had penetrating wounds in his hands and feet. He also has a wound in his side and bleeding around his head. The blood is human blood of a definite blood type which is the same type as that on the *suderion*, the face cloth which is kept in Avila in Spain. The *suderion* does not have an image on it. The image on the larger cloth in Turin, is not painted and is very superficial on the surface of the cloth. It is alleged, and firmly believed by many, to be the burial cloth of Jesus. How the image was produced on the cloth is not easy to determine, but its confinement to the surface fibers of the cloth and other features suggest that it was produced by some form of nuclear energy such as might have been produced by a molecular transformation of a human body. Another peculiarity of the image is that it is holistic and can be presented as a three dimensional figure, which distinguishes it from an ordinary photograph and again suggests some form of nuclear energy.

The shroud first showed up in modern times in the Cathedral of Turin in the thirteenth century, where it had been placed by Margaret de Charnay and it had apparently been in the possession of the de Charnay family for a considerable time. One of their ancestors had been preceptor for Normandy of the knights of the Temple (Templars). The Templars it is suggested obtained the shroud during the battles around Jerusalem during the crusades and may have used it in worship.[5] Its history before that is somewhat uncertain but it may have been in the possession of King Abda IV of Edessa who had it sent to Jerusalem when his kingdom became involved in wars and he feared for its safety.[6]

Many early Christian representations of Jesus appear to have been modeled on the shroud image, notably one in the orthodox monastery on Mount Sinai. Professor Ian Wilson, who first saw the shroud aged 14 and a confirmed agnostic, became fascinated by it and eventually became a Christian from studying it. He is particularly interested in the shroud's early history, especially the portraits of Jesus produced in the early centuries of the Christian era. He has documented about fifteen common features of these early pictures, noting many features that would have been unknown to artists who had not seen the shroud. He especially noted a box-like shape on the forehead which may well have been a *phylactery* containing quotations from the law which was worn by devout Jews.

---

[5] The Templars it seems were accused of worshipping a head which may have been the head of the shroud figure with the cloth folded up.

[6] The story goes that King Abda was very ill and sent messengers requesting that Jesus come and heal him. But Jesus was already crucified, resurrected and had subsequently left the earth, so they sent him the shroud instead and he was instantly healed.

The current skeptical view of the shroud is that it is a thirteenth century forgery, which seems implausible given that it explains few of its notable features. The skeptical opinion is based on the carbon dating of a tiny specimen of the shroud which indicated that it was produced in the thirteenth century. The taking of the sample and its preparation, or lack of it, for the test are well documented. It was necessary to avoid places where the shroud had been rewoven following damage by fire (reportedly in the thirteenth century). It was also important to clean the specimen for the shroud had been subjected to smoke damage and other forms of contamination. None of this was done and the general opinion is that the testing was badly mismanaged. Some, supporting the test, point out that the specimen was sent to three different laboratories with the same result. The uniform result is, however, hardly surprising since the three pieces were all part of the same specimen.

The question, then, is also whether anyone in the thirteenth century, or indeed any other, could have produced the shroud images. A number of features of the shroud image that we've noted argue for its authenticity.

- It is certainly not painted and the image is on the very surface of the fibers, not penetrating more deeply.
- The image can be used to produce a three dimensional holistic figure.
- There are pollen particles in the linen which have been shown, by a leading Jewish botanist, to be from flowers that grow near Jerusalem in the spring.
- Some of these pollens are from a plant which might have been used for a crown of thorns.

Photographic analysis and enhancement of the images show flowers and also the shape of a "crown of thorns," which relate to the Jewish custom, unknown later, of including flowers with the body. The "crown of thorns" would also have been included in what was buried since it would have had blood on the thorns.

A number of images of other artefacts have also been observed. Of particular interest is a box like shape and a spoon, which would have been used to pick up any blood spilled, since the blood was considered to be part of the body.

It is also notable that the nail prints are not in the middle of the palm where Christian art shows them, but in the correct location in the carpal bones of the wrist. If it had been otherwise the nails would have been torn through the flesh by the weight of the body.

In evaluating the shroud much depends on the perspectives the observer brings to it. If they are skeptical about religion, and especially if they incline to a vertical logic type of proof, they are very likely to assume a negative or at best an agnostic position on the matter. They may seek for any other explanation or fall back on the Scottish criminal verdict of "not proven".

Could any forger in the thirteenth century or of any other have known all this and included it in the image?

Many people who have looked at the image thoughtfully and been aware of all these things, like Professor Ian Wilson, have been inclined to believe that it is the burial shroud of Jesus.

SUGGESTIONS FOR FURTHER READING

Benedict XVI, Pope. *Jesus of Nazareth*. New York: Doubleday, 2007. Print.

Wilson, Ian. *The Shroud of Turin: The Burial Cloth of Jesus Christ?* Garden City, N.Y.: Doubleday, 1978. Print.

Wilson, Ian. *The Shroud: The 2000-year Old Mystery Solved*. London: Bantam, 2010. Print. Baillie, D. M. *God Was in Christ: an Essay on Incarnation and Atonement*. New York: C. Scribner's Sons, 1948. Print.

Flew, R. Newton. *Jesus and His Church: A Study of the Idea of the Ecclesia in the New Testament*. New York: Abingdon, 1938. Print.

Duguid, Iain M. *Is Jesus in the Old Testament?* Phillipsburg, NJ: P & R, 2013. Print.

The "Christology" article on Wikipedia covers the early controversies in the church quite well.

Brunner, Emil. *The Mediator: A Study of the Central Doctrine of the Christian Faith*. Philadelphia: Westminster, 1947. Print.

V

Thinking about the Holy Spirit

The Holy Spirit is often taken to be a synonym for God immanent and active in our lives. But in the Bible, and especially in the New Testament, the Spirit of God is viewed as a distinct person; and this is especially clear in the Fourth Gospel where the Spirit is promised to come when Jesus is ascended into Heaven. This refers us back to the difficult question of the Trinity, a notion which we've seen is not easy to express in rational terms, and which we thought about in particular in chapter three on God.

More practical questions though arise in relation to the activity of the Spirit in our own lives. In the Old Testament, special persons were appointed by God, or perhaps we should say anointed by God, to declare His will to His people. Moses, it is said in the Book of Deuteronomy was the greatest of all prophets to whom God spoke face to face with as a man speaks to his friend (Exod 33:11). Later on the "sons of the prophets", a group of persons especially devoted to God, are mentioned though with little detail as to how or when they spoke for God. (2 Kings 2:4-7) The presence of the Spirit in them was shown by ecstatic behavior especially dancing. David danced before the Lord when the ark was being returned to Jerusalem. (2 Sam 6:14) In the Acts of the Apostles the coming of the promised Holy Spirit was authenticated in a remarkable miracle where the visitors to Jerusalem each heard the words of the apostles in their own native tongue. (Acts 2:8).[1] This miracle, which signified the spreading of the Gospel to every nation, is quite different from the speaking in tongues (*glossolalia*) that we meet in the early church, since it did not require an interpreter. But receiving the Holy Spirit in some manner or other was considered the mark of salvation, a

---

[1] An unfortunate title perhaps for a book which says little about any of the apostles other than Peter and Paul and more accurately described in Luke's own words as the story of what Jesus continued to do in his Body, the Church.

necessary sign that one had become one of the people of God. St. Peter reported of his activity with gentiles that they received the Holy Spirit just as we did, (Acts 10:47) and the same was held to authenticate the preaching of the Gospel to gentiles generally. And this is further described by saying that they spoke ecstatically in an unknown tongue. St. Paul found a group of persons who had only had the baptism of John and he asked them did they receive the Holy Spirit when they believed. They replied that they had not even heard that there was a Holy Spirit (Acts 19:2). Paul instructed them more adequately and baptized them in the name of Jesus and they then spoke in tongues showing that they had received the Spirit.

Speaking in tongues (*glossalalia* in Greek) was a common occurrence in the early church, but it had its problems and St. Paul had to rein it in, requiring that someone interpret the message (1 Cor 14:18–40). This must have reduced the frequency of the practice a good deal as an interpreter was not always available. Paul's final conclusions on this topic are interesting and important. In the twelfth and thirteenth chapters of his first letter to the Corinthians he expresses his concerns about the *glossolalia* in Christian worship. He says that anyone visiting might think they were all drunk or mad, and he goes on to show a more excellent way of demonstrating the presence of the Spirit in our lives. The presence of the Spirit is shown, he says, by three gifts, those of *faith*, *hope* and *love*. All of these are gifts, not achievements. True faith, where belief in God and Christ is real and living in our deepest being, is a gift that arrives when Christ enters our lives. Similarly hope, the confidence that our future is in God's hands and that he works all things together for good, is also a gift to us. And love, the most important sign of all, is the final gift that arrives. This is not an emotional surge, though emotion is often involved. It is rather the turning of our natures inside out, so that we become concerned about other people rather than ourselves. The arrival of these things in our lives is the work of the Spirit and tells us that we are truly born of God and His children (Rom 8:16).

But this is not to say that speaking in tongues is forbidden, only that it is not the only way nor necessarily the best way to express the presence of the Holy Spirit in our lives. A number of my friends, Pentecostals and others, speak in tongues. They describe this as an experience where human language cannot express their joy, and a special tongue is provided. But they tend to exercise this gift in private during their own devotions rather than in public.

Pentecostal Churches

Pentecostalism is both a church (or a group of churches) and a movement inside other churches. Pentecostals tend to view themselves as restoring the apostolic type of Christianity found in the New Testament. Pentecostalism emerged in the twentieth century from the holiness movement which has its roots in Methodism. A revivalist preacher and faith healer Charles Parham began teaching in Los Angeles at the beginning of the twentieth century that the baptism of the Holy Spirit was the scriptural sign of conversion and was evidenced by speaking in tongues and also miraculous healing. A three-year long Azuza Street revival in Los Angeles followed and began a spread of Pentecostal ideas both in the United States and even further afield around the world, as Pentecostal missionaries carried the message to every country that they could. There are estimated to be over 700 separate Pentecostal groups worldwide besides independent churches. There is no central authority in the Pentecostal movement but many of these groups are affiliated with the Pentecostal World Fellowship. Pentecostal ideas have also taken root in more mainline Protestant and Catholic churches. The *charismatic movement*, as it is often referred to, of Pentecostal Christians of one sort or another, are estimated to number around five hundred million people worldwide. It should also be noted that there is considerable variety within this body and that there are Pentecostal churches that do not speak in tongues although firmly believing and trusting in being filled with the Holy Spirit in ways described in the Acts of the Apostles.

On Casting Lots and Corporate Decisions

It is appropriate here to make some comments on the matter of casting lots. In the Old Testament the stones Urim and Thumim were cast to decide who should be King (1 Sam 14:41) and also to determine just who was the sinner that was causing trouble to fall on Israel (Josh 7:1). The lot was later used to decide which of the disciples was to replace Judas as one of the twelve (Acts 1:26). The lot is still used among Mennonite Christians to decide which of several candidates shall be their Bishop. This sounds like a sort of divine gambling but it is always proceeded among the Mennonites by a considerable amount of prayer. Most Christians leave out the lot and focus on prayer alone when faced with choices, which is all well and good provided the will of God is earnestly sought and it is not replaced by simply relying on our own wit and knowledge.

Indeed, the Holy Spirit is also linked in the New Testament to corporate decisions and activities in the Church as a body. When it was decided by the Church in Antioch to send missionaries to the gentiles they prayed earnestly and concluded by saying that "it seemed good to the Holy Spirit and us" (Acts 15:28). Paul and his companions were also blocked by the Spirit when they sought to take their missionary activity in one direction rather than another (Acts 15:6). Precisely how the Spirit communicated His will to the Church is something of a mystery here and always, but the will of the Spirit should be sought with the expectation that communication to His Church, by one means or another, will be found.

SUGGESTIONS FOR FURTHER READING

A very thorough article covering modern Pentecostal churches and charismatic movements within other churches can be found in Wikipedia under the title "Pentecostal."

Synan, Vinson. *The Holiness-Pentecostal Tradition: Charismatic Movements in the Twentieth Century.* Grand Rapids: Eerdmans, 1997. Print. This contains a full description of holiness/Pentecostal movements in non-Pentecostal churches, including the earlier roots of the movement in Methodism.

Arthur, William. *The Tongue of Fire.* New York: Harper & Bros., 1880. Print. This is a classic presentation by a great Methodist scholar of a former generation.

Pinnock, Clark H. *The Flame of Love: A Theology of the Holy Spirit.* Downers Grove: InterVarsity Press, 1996. Print.

VI

Thinking about Man, Sin, and Salvation

"The chief end of man is to glorify God and enjoy Him forever"
(Westminster Shorter Catechism)

"What is man?" is a philosophical question. It cannot be answered by a study of facts alone, nor by statistical studies or factual studies of any other kind. One must think conceptually and horizontally by applying one notion after another until we find one that fits best for the purposes and goals we have in mind when we are asking the question. In this chapter and to this end, we will look at the Biblical picture or rather Biblical pictures of man, for there can be more than one way to characterize the Biblical account of mankind.

First a note on the gender question may be helpful. Hebrew uses the term *Adam* for mankind in general, including both males and females. If man as male is intended, a different word, *Ish*, is used. Most languages make this distinction and have separate words for mankind in general (males and females together) and for the singular (man or woman), but English does not. The same word "man" covers both ideas. By the term "man" then, here and throughout this book, unless otherwise specified it will signify mankind, including both males and females.

Perhaps the most basic and important set of ideas about mankind are found in the Genesis account of creation where man (Adam) is made in the image and likeness of God. There are two separate accounts of this event. The first, found in chapter one of Genesis, states that God made mankind (Adam) from Adamah (the earth) in his image and likeness, male (*ish*) and female (*ishah*) HE created *them*. The second chapter of Genesis has a more imaginative account, a sort of story logic even, where man is made out of the dust of the ground, God breathes into his nostrils the breath of life, and man becomes a living soul (*nephesh*). *Nephesh* simply means breathing and life. Soul in our sense, the part that survives death, is most often called *spirit* in the Bible, (*ruach*).[1] God then creates woman (*eva'*) to be a companion for man, and also to be the mother of mankind (*eva* means mother), and places them both in a beautiful garden to tend and look after it.[2]

What is this image and likeness of God? It is said of no other creature except man, and is not further explained in Genesis. But some qualities of God are revealed in these accounts. Through them we know that God is creator and therefore also creative. He is good and knows what is good, and the term good here does not only mean morally good but also aesthetically good, as in beautiful. So God is an innovative creator and an artist with a sense of beauty. He appreciates and cares for His creation. His goodness then includes affection and love. These qualities man alone shares with his Creator.[3] And the man (here in the singular sense) is also incomplete without woman. She is fashioned from a rib taken from his own body (the first thoracotomy under anesthesia) and Adam declares that she is "bone of my bone and flesh of my flesh".[4] The Biblical idea of marriage follows from this, for it is said "therefore shall a man leave his father and mother and cleave to his wife and they shall be one flesh," as in one body, or person. (Gen 2:24) The purpose of creating man becomes clear when we hear that God walks in the cool of the evening with the first humans (Gen 3:18), it is fellowship, where like shares with like.

But the Genesis account also talks of the fall of man from this first place of privilege (in Genesis 3) The tempter is represented

---

[1] The Hebrew term *ruach* also describes the powerful desert wind. It thus speaks of great power that we can neither predict nor control. You may remember that the coming of the Holy Spirit on the day of Pentecost in Acts 2 was accompanied by a rushing mighty wind.

[2] The term paradise was originally the name for the great pleasure parks of the Persian Kings.

[3] Affection can be found in a vestigial form in higher mammals, a sign of God's creating hand at work.

[4] Quoted by Jesus in answer to the question put to him by the Pharisees about divorce (Mark 1:1-12).

by the serpent, and the temptation is to eat the forbidden fruit, the result of which is expulsion from the garden and a series of curses on all the guilty parties including the ground. What is so terrible, one wonders, about taking fruit from the tree, many of us "progged" orchards in our time and didn't think it a capital offense. But the tree is symbolic, it is the tree of knowing good and evil. This too might seem a good thing, but what is intended here is to seek knowledge like that of God, deciding what is good and what is evil for oneself. It is usurping God's place and setting ourselves up as our own authority, independent of God. It is described by various words in the Bible; as *transgression* (breaking the law); *rebellion*; and *pride*, the puffing up of ourselves with our own importance. All of these amount to the same thing, putting oneself in the place that properly belongs to God. And bad things follow. It is not long in the book of Genesis before we hear of the first murder, and a little later of Lamech boasting to his two wives that he had killed a younger man. And soon we come to Sodom and Gomorrah, the cities of the plain, where every kind of depravity was normal everyday living. The message of Genesis is that from the first great sin all sorts of others follow. Cut off from his Maker man rots and the rot spreads and gets worse from generation to generation.

Original Sin

This brings us to the doctrine of original sin. St. Augustine linked this to being conceived in sin, created by the sexual act which, though permissible, is in itself sinful. This is an odd notion, for it never occurred to Moses or the prophets, or any other Old Testament writers that sex was in itself wrongful. It was given and commanded by God who told us to be fruitful and multiply and replenish the earth; and to make it work God made it a source of pleasure and joy saying "rejoice O man with the wife of thy youth and take delight in her breasts" (Eccl 11:9).[5] Admittedly this can be tempered is we remember that the Psalmist said "in sin did my mother conceive me," but he was beating his breast at the

---

[5] One of John Wesley's solemn preachers complained that Mr. Wesley tempted him to levity with his little jokes. Wesley replied that he found it impossible to be solemn all the time since God had linked all good things to pleasure.

time having committed both the despicable murder of his loyal follower Uriah the Hittite and adultery with Uriah's wife. So the expression should be taken as more figurative rather than a statement of absolute fact. The Syrian Orthodox (Antiochine) Church view is surely better balanced and more in accord with scripture.[6] This locates original sin in the fact that we are inevitably social beings, linked to one another for good or ill, so that by being born into the human race we inherit its twistedness as well as its benefits. This fits in with what St. Paul's says about our inheriting a sinful nature from the first Adam which leads to death, but our spiritual Nature we receive from the second Adam, Christ, in whom we are made alive (1 Cor 15:45). The idea here is that there are two streams of humanity. That flowing from the first Adam provides us all with our sinful warped aspects, all that we were not meant to be, and we simply cannot escape it. When we are born into a Christian home or otherwise find our way into the Church, we are placed into a second more profitable stream, the heritage of the second Adam, Christ, which leads to life. This is the stream of grace, flowing from Christ, in the Christian home and the Church, which carries with it blessings rather than curses. But we travel through life in both streams. Even though we are in the stream that leads to life we are also born into a human family with its own burden of defects. And even if our family were faultless, we have to go to school and later out into the world and get our already stained and torn clothing messed up even worse. But fortunately we can be introduced into the Church of Christ, His body on earth. This is the notion that lies behind the practice of baptizing infants. We are not performing spiritual chemistry on them, but introducing them into the realm and stream of grace.

Total Depravity

We come now to the doctrine of total depravity, beloved of John Calvin and John Wesley and evangelical preachers generally. It is hinted at even in the communion service that "there is no health

---

[6] A Syrian Orthodox (Antiochine) priest, a Billy Graham convert no less, expounded this notion at an ecumenical minsters' meeting in South Down during my sojourn as a Methodist minister in the Newcastle Circuit.

in us." The reason for the doctrine's popularity with evangelistic preachers is that it completely cuts the ground from beneath any suggestion that we might be good enough for heaven as we are, without Christ, on the merits of our good behavior. The notion of total depravity springs from a number of verses in the Bible. Some of them are poetic such as "I am a worm and not a man" (Ps 22:6), or where Isaiah says that "all our righteousness is as filthy rags" (Is 64:6), which is merely to say what Job said, when he finally saw God, that he "abhorred himself in dust and ashes" (Job 46:2). All these simply mean that in the presence of God our pretenses to righteousness fade away into nothing by comparison. Other texts are clearer, as when Paul argues that our works constitute no claim to salvation. And all of this is true but falls short of the evidence required for the notion of total depravity. Jesus taught us that our good deeds do not provide merit, for when the disciples claimed that they had left all they had to follow him (their "what's in it for us?" moment), He told them they would be well rewarded even in this life but added, "When you have done all, say we are unprofitable servants we only did our duty" (Luke 17:10). It is impossible for us, it seems, to do more than our duty and not look to score points for it. In fact we usually spoil our good deeds by giving ourselves a congratulatory pat on the back. But this does not mean that there is nothing good left in us since the fall into sin. Sin is a separation from God which sets us, and all that we are, off on the wrong track. We still may have, and usually do have, some good things about us, commonly due to the fact that we have been well brought up; and a little of this good inheritance sticks even when we do not have the faith of our fathers and mothers. Unfortunately it tends to wither away, a little more perhaps with each generation. It is hardly something then, for which we can claim credit but it benefits us none the less and all those about us. We do not have to pretend that we have secret evil motives in asserting and even practicing these good values. It is just that they do not chalk up any points in our favor that can accumulate and ultimately exempt us from the need to be saved. And when we return to God these good things that were lying dormant in us are awakened. As the hymn writer put it:

> Down in the human heart crushed by the Tempter
> Feelings lie buried that grace can restore
> Touched by a loving hand wakened by kindness
> Chords that were broken may vibrate once more.

God does not check our accounts for good deeds to see if we are worthy of salvation, but he does check our accounts (1 Cor 3:15) and the psalms make it clear that the Lord delights in us when we are doing things right.[7] While it is true that we are not saved by good works, we are saved so that we may perform good works, so that the purpose of our salvation is to produce good deeds (Eph 2:8–9) and these are pleasing to God.

The Evil Consequences of the Fall

It might be a good thing to return for a moment to the evils which followed the fall of man (so back to Gen 3). The curse which followed human rebellion fell first on Adam himself. He would be forced to make a living the hard way, he would provide for himself and his family in sorrow and with the sweat of his brow. The curse of woman would be in the pains of childbirth and also that she would be under the heel of her stronger partner.[8] Even the ground was cursed. This seems an odd notion till we remember that sinful man abuses the earth instead of nurturing it, polluting its waters and wiping out its creatures in an unending search for gain. But in Christ these curses are removed. Work is redeemed, it can become an opportunity to do good and an interesting and enjoyable occupation. The curse on womankind is likewise removed in Christ. The birth of the baby is anticipated with pleasure and when it is born the pains of childbirth are forgotten "for joy that a child has come into the world" (John 16:21). The relation of man and woman is also redeemed as they are now

---

[7] Isaac Watts has it,
"What is the creature's skill or force, the sprightly man the warlike horse,
The piercing wit, the active limb, are all too mean delights for him.
–But saints are lovely in his sight, He views his children with delight.
He sees their hopes He knows their fears and looks and loves his image there".

[8] This is the meaning of the expression "your desire shall be unto him." In other words, you will do whatever he wants.

one person. The question of who is boss is moot and irrelevant as the two seek as a team to do God's will. Even the curse on the ground is removed as we see our calling to nurture and care for it. Retracing our steps to return to God reverses all the curses and replaces them with blessings.

Salvation

The doctrine of salvation follows from that of sin. Sin is separation from God with its consequences. Salvation is the same thing in reverse, reunion with God and the things that follow from that. But it is not so much our returning to God, it is rather God seeking and finding us.[9] The Shepherd is seeking the lost sheep till be finds it. One point that must be remembered here is that, unlike the lost sheep, we are not entirely passive. We must actively respond to the grace of God. The lost prodigal must come to himself and turn to the father. But when he does the Father runs to meet him. The prodigal is back in the family. He receives a ring on his finger and new clothes. The occasion is celebrated with a feast, the fatted calf is killed and there is music and joyful dancing. As Jesus said, there is joy in heaven when a sinner repents and is restored. But the parable says nothing of what follows. Were there no consequences of his folly? That would require another parable and is the subject of the chapter dealing with the Christian life.

The Atonement

The saving work of Christ on the Cross has always been a particularly difficult thing to explain. For how can the death of one person accrue to the benefit of all others? Critics have viewed this doctrine as a reading back into the gospels of St. Paul's attempt to explain why God allowed Jesus to die. The original Jesus of Nazareth, it is argued, was a prophet with a new and unpopular way of explaining the kingly rule of God. His death was not an atoning sacrifice but rather a deliberate acceptance of the

---

[9] Both are found in the Gospels, the prodigal son says "I will arise and go to my father" (who runs to meet him), and the good shepherd goes forth to find the lost sheep.

inevitable consequence of his opposition to the harsh religion of the Jews, at the hands of the Romans; in short a martyrdom. Its saving effect is in our accepting his invitation to follow in His pathway. But, as is often the case, getting rid of one problem only leads to creating other more difficult ones. Dr. Vincent Taylor, in his two great works on this subject (*Jesus and His Sacrifice* and *The Atonement in the New Testament Teaching*) has clearly shown that no matter how far you go back or how deeply you dig in the New Testament teaching, the idea of the sacrificial work of Christ is always present. One third of Mark's gospel is devoted to this topic and it is obvious that it was a vital part of Jesus perception of his own destiny and purpose. But having said this, we have still not explained it or greatly increased our understanding of it, in any significant way. Church fathers and major theologians have sought to present it in a variety of ways. In the first few centuries of the Christian era the atonement was seen as a great victory over the enemies of God, in particular the devil.[10] Sometimes this was spelled out in terms that seem crude, even ridiculous to us today, an example being that the devil was fooled into taking Jesus in exchange for us as it seemed like a good bargain at the time, but then he found that he could not hold Him and so was cheated out of his prey. Generally, however, the victory theory was taken more sensibly to mean that Jesus in His life and death conquered death and sin and that, united with Him, we reap the benefits of this victory. How this happens is not exactly clear but it could be taken to mean that by giving ourselves over to Him we are victorious with Him.

Later the death of Jesus was seen in feudal terms as preserving God's honor, which had been besmirched by our sinning against His law. Another approach is to say that God must be consistent in his actions, so He cannot just easily forgive sins which he has already outlawed with attached penalties. He cannot simply say that the laws will no longer be enforced as if they no longer existed. The penalties must somehow be paid and since we cannot pay them ourselves, God must himself take the matter in hand.

In the New Testament itself, Jesus atoning death is seen in

---

[10] See Gustav Aulen, *Christus Victor* (1974).

terms of the sacrifice for sin prescribed in the law, with some differences, for Jesus alone is the only truly acceptable sacrifice in this case. The sacrificial animal had to be without blemish but Jesus was more than this, He was without sin. Furthermore the Mosaic sacrifice for sin had to be repeated, but the sacrifice of Jesus was accomplished once and for all time (Rom 6:10).[11]

The term "atonement" is used in the New Testament to describe Jesus' sacrificial death. This is sometimes rendered as equivalent to *at-one-ment*, of bringing opposed parties together. But this is a comment on the English word, not an account of the original Hebrew term (*kaphoreth*) which is derived from a root meaning "covering," as in to cover over one's sins seen in the related Jewish feast of *Yom Kippur*. In Jewish commentary this involved repentance, restitution and a sacrificial gift. This can be understood as being like a Hebrew penitent laying his hand on the sacrificial animal as a sign that he is giving himself along with it (a "me too"). So in much the same way one can hope to appropriate to oneself the sacrificial gift of Jesus.

St. Paul adds to these ideas somewhat by saying that Christ nailed our sins and transgressions with his own body on the tree and goes on to add that in Christ we must likewise die to sin and be resurrected to newness of life. He describes us as being buried with Christ in baptism and raised with him into newness of life. He even speaks of his own frequent and very severe sufferings as filling up anything that was lacking in Christ's suffering.

These various formal expressions suggest ways in which the death of Jesus may be understood to allow forgiveness of our sins and restore us to God, but generally without moving the matter much further than the original statements of the New Testament. When I have asked older and wiser persons to explain it to me, I noticed that they always held their head between their hands and screwed up their face, which suggested to me that they were engaged in very strenuous thinking on a most difficult matter. But though it cannot be well explained, the event is clearly spelled out in the New Testament so that we can believe, and appreciate

---

[11] The comparison of the perfect sacrifice of Jesus with those provided in the Mosaic Law is spelled out in some detail in the Epistle to the Hebrews, chapter 7.

Jesus' sacrifice for us even though we only dimly understand it. Indeed, it is made real for us in the central ritual of our worship, the Lord's Supper. When we receive the poured out wine and eat the broken bread, we reenact Christ's suffering, and we take into our deepest being what Christ has obtained for us by his passion.

SUGGESTIONS FOR FURTHER READING

Taylor, Vincent. *The Atonement in New Testament Teaching*. Eugene, Ore.: Wipf & Stock, 2009. Print.

"Atonement in Christianity," on Wikipedia, offers a lengthy article on this topic. See also their article "Sacrifice in the Old Testament."

Smith, Charles Ryder, *The Bible Doctrine of Man*. London: Epworth, 1951. Print. A well-known treatment on this topic.

Kelsey, David H. *Imagining Redemption*. Louisville: Westminster John Knox Press, 2005. Print.

The articles on and related to "Anthropology" on Wikipedia were overly technical.

VII

Thinking about the Church

In the country churches of North Carolina, the members call the church building the Church House. When a visiting minister wondered about this they told him, "We are the Church, that's the Church House". And they were right. The Church in the New Testament is described as a body or a building made up of the various members who are like the organs of the body or stones which make up a building. The members, taken together, form the Church.

In the New Testament the term for the church is *ecclesia*. This word is taken from the Greek version of the Old Testament (the LXX) where it is used for the Hebrew term *qahal*, translated "the assembly" in the English Bible. Both signify a group of people called together. And that is what the church is, a body of people called together by Christ.

In addition to body and building, the church is described in the New Testament even as a flock. And a flock is not a particularly nice word or image unless there is a shepherd looking after it. Jesus wept over the people of Jerusalem because they were like sheep without a shepherd. (Luke 19:41–44) But His flock are guarded by the Good Shepherd (John 19:11), and He said to the first group of disciples "fear not little flock it is your Father's good pleasure to give you the Kingdom" (Luke 12:32).

Built on a Rock

The most important passage of scripture concerning the Church is found in Matthew chapter 16. The disciples had been taken to the remote area of Caesarea Philippi, where Jesus, having been with them for a considerable time, tested their understanding of who He was. He began by asking them, "Who do men say that I am?" The disciples responded by giving him various answers, "some say this and some say that." Then Jesus asked the crucial question, "Who do you say I am?", and Peter gave the right answer, "You are the Christ, the Son of the Living God". Jesus then explained to him, "You did not come to this conclusion on your own. It was revealed to you by God," and he went on to say, "You are Peter, and on this rock I will build my Church and the Gates of Hades shall not prevail against it. And I will give you the keys of the Kingdom and whatever you bind on earth shall be bound in Heaven."

This passage has become a theological battle ground. The Roman Catholic Church interprets it as making Peter the Vicar of Christ on earth with the various succeeding Bishops of Rome as his legitimate successors, who thereby inherit his powers and authority.

The reformers, not surprisingly, noted that the Roman Church claim is a considerable stretch on the original grant; for it is not said that the bishops of Rome or anywhere else are Peter's successors. Protestants have therefore interpreted the text somewhat differently. Many have viewed Peter as one rock and the other rock as his confession, noting that the gender of the word "Peter" and that of the word "rock" is different in Greek, so the church is built on his confession rather than Peter personally. Unfortunately for this view the gender distinction between this Rock (Peter) and the other Rock (supposedly his confession) does not hold in Aramaic, the language that Jesus spoke.

Building on Rabbinic Wisdom

Dr. Robert Newton Flew, one of the ablest theologians that Methodism or anybody else produced in the last century, has a different account of this saying.[1] Dr. Flew was notable for his knowledge of the rabbinical literature, and his use of it in interpreting the New Testament. The rabbis, Flew tells us, spoke of Israel as a building and also believed that it was founded on a rock. The saying goes that "God wishing to build his house sought a rock for its foundation, and that rock was Abraham". The thought here was not that anyone would rule in Abraham's shoes, but that God's

---

[1] See Flew's, *Jesus and His Church*, especially chapter 4.

house was built of believers, Abraham being the first believer and thus the first stone. All the later believers were built on top of him. With this in mind then in Christian terms, Peter was the first to believe, and the rest are built on top of him to form God's house. It was not Peter's faith that was the original foundation of the Church it was Peter as the first believer. This fits in well with St. Paul's saying that the Church was built on the foundation of the Apostles and Prophets and you (his hearers) are added on as living stones with Jesus Christ as the chief corner stone (that holds it all together; Eph 2:20).

Dr. Flew's exposition of the rest of this passage is equally interesting. The gates of Hades are the gates of death, and, in short His Church will never die, and it never has.[2] The keys of the Kingdom are the signs of authority, and are given to all believers not just to Peter who happened to be the first one. Dr. Flew also points out that the gift of the keys can be used to admit people to the kingdom, not only to keep them out. Binding and loosing are also rabbinical expressions, and were used of each rabbi's authority to bind the consciences of their flock by his interpretation of the law. There is an old rabbinical tale about a Jewish fine food enthusiast who found a wonderful recipe for roasted peacock that was prepared and then served up with the feathers and skin put back on again. But a doubt is said to have struck him and he asked his rabbi whether a peacock was a clean or unclean bird. The rabbi said it was unclean. The foodie said, "Thank you rabbi, I will destroy it." But the rabbi stopped him and said, "No, give it to me and I'll eat it." "But rabbi you said it was unclean." The rabbi answered, "That is my opinion, and since I am your rabbi you cannot eat it; but my father is my rabbi and he thinks this sort of bird is clean, so I can eat it." And while an old story, this powerfully illustrates how binding and loosing could operate. Transposing this, binding and loosing would then be the power of the church to bind the consciences of its people and indeed of the world at large The right to this binding power of course depends on the Church seeking the will of God and not being moved by interest or favor. This is not to say that every policy

---

[2] Hades was the realm of the dead; the place we call Hell, *the valley of Hinnom*, which takes its name from the rubbish heap outside Jerusalem.

statement of the Church is correct but that when Christian people have definitely come as a matter of clear conscience to the conclusion that something is right and should be done; or wrong so that it shouldn't, then the power of heaven is behind them.

What then is the Church? The Free Church of Scotland Catechism, states that the church is that community where the true Gospel is preached and the sacraments are duly administered.[3] I am sure that this is largely true but it is not quite what the New Testament says. The letters of John were written when the fledgling Christian Churches were encountering a serious problem. Roving teachers were traveling round with letters of introduction supposedly from the Apostles in Jerusalem. But they were really heretics, coming like wolves among the flock. The test proposed by John to detect these interlopers was that if they believe and say that Jesus is the Christ, they are to be received and helped on their way. If not, they were to be avoided and sent packing The writer of John's letters goes on to say many things about the true faith that its teachers must hold fast to. It is not a mere doctrinal formula, a train of ideas in the head (as Mr. Wesley would say), but also a disposition of the heart, and whoever believes this in their heart is born of God (Rom 10:9). If we go further and apply this to our understanding of the Church, then the Church is a body who believe that Jesus is the Christ, the Son of God.

The Catholic Church

The Apostle's and the Nicene Creed both speak of the Holy Catholic Church. But *catholic* means worldwide, the whole as opposed to particular parts, or the church in some locality. Seen in this light the Church is made up of many groups and denominations with different views on many things. It therefore includes Pentecostals, Catholics of various kinds, Presbyterians, Congregationalists, Quakers (who do not administer the sacraments), Methodists (of course), and any others who believe as the apostles did that Jesus is the Christ. All these groups are themselves composed of living stones built into God's building on the same foundation. Together they make up the Catholic

---

[3] See here the *Shorter Catechism*, Question 35.

Church which will never die: and it will open the gates of Heaven to all who will believe, and speak in God's name on matters of right and wrong. When we declare that we believe in the Holy Catholic church we are reaching out to our fellow Christians of every kind around the world.

This is not to say that our differences are not important. Roman Catholics believe that it is necessary to submit to the Bishop of Rome. High church Anglicans believe that the church must trace its descent through a proper succession of bishops going back to the Apostles, the so called *apostolic succession*, taken up below. Fervent evangelicals will doubt the credentials of any church that does not match up to the pattern of beliefs that they feel the church should have. But these differences, important as they are to us, are not critical. The revival of an interest in the Bible has allowed us to focus on the things that we hold in common and encourages us to seek God's guidance on the differences. I have been reading two books by the recently resigned Pope Benedict XVI. I was amazed and delighted to find how slight our differences are, and how these differences mattered little to the heart of our shared faith; indeed, how my heart warmed to what he was saying. [4] As Mr. Wesley remarked in his sermon on the catholic spirit, "if your heart is as my heart give me your hand" (quoting and misapplying the words of Jehu, son of Nimshi, recorded in 2 Kings 10:15).

Church in Practice

Before moving to some extended thinking on some of the matters just raised I would like to offer a few practical points which spring from thinking about the Church.

First of all, we should try to remember that the Church and congregation to which we belong is Christ's body, it is God's house. When we go to worship there, Christ has promised to meet with us should only two or three persons be present. We come to meet the Lord, and Worship is not meant as a spectator

---

[4] The books were his, *Jesus of Nazareth* (a marvelous book) and *Dogma and Preaching* (heavier going but excellent none the less). We differed on the meaning of tradition (see my chapter "Thinking about the Bible"); we differed less on the subject of the Virgin Mary than I had anticipated.

sport. We sing to God, Mr. Wesley urging us to sing heartily and in time (not necessarily in tune for that may not be our gift). When we begin to pray, pray, rather than wander. The minister leads the Church in prayer, and we should follow this lead, and we should also pray for the Church in our own devotions as well. When it comes to preaching we should be expecting God to say something to us, In fact we should not just be listening *to* the sermon, but also listening *through* the proclaimed word, trying to hear God's message for each of us.

Second, we should look on one another very kindly. We are but flesh and blood; ordinary and fallible people whom God has called into his Church. We sometimes expect too much of one another. We carry the divine treasure in earthen vessels (2 Cor 4:7) and so we need to be more understanding and forgiving, remembering our own shortcomings.

Third, remember that the Church, as an item in the Creed, is an article of faith. We do not see all of it with our eyes. The Church is visible, but if we only see what our eyes and ears tell us we have not seen all there is. If we only see the outward persons there with us in church, we are not seeing them as we should and as they truly are. So when we look on the body with our eyes, we also need to see it by faith, knowing that Christ is present in us and with us. This should make us careful about what we say or do. When St. Paul commented on some people misbehaving at the Lord's Supper, he said that they were not seeing the Lord's body, they were only seeing bread and wine. When we remember that Christ is there with us, we will behave accordingly.

The Apostolic Succession

Many churches, including the Roman Catholic, Orthodox, Anglican and some Lutherans, hold that the continuity of the Church with the Church of the apostolic age is guaranteed by tracing the succession of bishops in unbroken line to the Apostles. In support of this position they cite that Paul laid hands on Timothy and that the apostles in turn consecrated others in every church that they established. Critics, and some of these are Roman Catholic theologians, are dubious about the scriptural foundations here, considering the apostolic practice to be a matter or order, putting some responsible person in charge of a new and fragile Christian congregation. There are also gaps in the tradition, for instance the Bishop of the Church of Alexandria was not considered to lack apostolicity because there was no record of a succession of episcopal ordinations but rather it was deemed to be a succession of elders. Also Irenaeus, writing in the later part of the second century refers to a succession of presbyters rather than bishops.[5]

But the main problem with the doctrine of apostolic succession is not historical but rather theological. It appears to be a rather mechanical way of ensuring the continuity of the tradition. Some Roman Catholic writers, while not opposing the doctrine, have voiced the same concern. Protestant churches have favored a more real continuity with Christ and the apostolic church, with continuity of the Church rather shown in maintaining the apostolic faith (especially faith in Christ as the Son of God). Some theologians have talked of the Evangelical Succession, from Paul, through Augustine and Luther to Wesley, which is really another argument for a continuity of belief.[6] Another mark of apostolicity can be seen in the continuing presence of the Holy Spirit dwelling in and guiding the Church, and this is manifested in maintaining fellowship with other churches who profess the same faith. The varieties of expression on this subject among various churches are legion, but the foregoing is a representative sampling.

Church Order

The Church is an organization and as such requires order; and order as well as discipline it had right from the beginning. After the early period when the twelve apostles were able to meet the formal needs of the church, a further arrangement was needed to take care of a crisis that had arisen concerning care for the unfortunate. The Jewish community took care of helpless people, widows, orphans and those handicapped by serious ailments and injured in accidents. They were supplied with food and money

---

[5] In reply it is argued that he terms presbyter and *episkopos* (bishop) are perhaps interchangeable.

[6] For one such example see Franz Hildebrandt's *From Luther to Wesley*. London: Lutterworth, 1951. Print.

which was collected every week. The Christian unfortunates were not considered eligible for the weekly Jewish allotment and so they organized their own. But a complaint arose that those widows who were of Greek and not Jewish origin, were not being helped, in short that they were being discriminated against by those organizing the weekly distribution. The apostles responded to this crisis by having seven officers chosen, called *deacons*, from a Greek word meaning a servant (Acts 6:1–6). Many of the seven deacons had Greek names, such as *Stephanos*, a wise move since they could be expected to give fair play to the Greek widows. And it would seem that they were men with other gifts besides administration, for we find Stephen preaching and arguing with the Jews, showing from the scriptures that Jesus was the Christ. And when we come to Phillip we encounter, more or less, a wandering missionary and evangelist.

As the church became established in the gentile world, other *offices* or *orders* developed. Elders were established in every congregation. An elder was more or less a reliable mature person who could be a shepherd of the congregation; and they were urged by New Testament writers to be faithful shepherds till the Good Shepherd would appear to reward them. Deacons also were mentioned in earlier sources, and we can assume that they were administrative officers of one kind or another as well.

In the letters of St. Paul and the other apostolic writers we find lists of people with God-given gifts that they used in the service of the Church. So St. Paul says that when Jesus ascended up on high he gave some to be apostles, some prophets, some evangelists some pastors and teachers for the perfecting of the saints, and some for the work of the ministry, and so on (Eph 4:8). There is some uncertainty as to what these persons were and how they operated. "Apostles" seems to indicate more than the twelve appointed by Jesus and, may have meant traveling teachers and evangelists whom we might now call missionaries. It is notable that there is no mention of preachers, but perhaps they were included under another name or heading such as prophets. A prophet was one who listened to God and then proclaimed what he had heard. In Deuteronomy it is said that no prophet has since arisen like Moses who talked with God face to face as a man talks with his friend. And that is exactly what a preacher is supposed to do. If this is so, it is notable that the evangelist Phillip had four daughters who were prophetesses (Acts 21:8), the first women preachers.

Later, organization in the church became more complex and more precisely defined. The membership of the Medieval Church, both Eastern and Western, was divided broadly into, priests and lay persons.[7] The priests themselves were divided into a number of orders themselves, including deacons, exorcists, and the like. And the lower orders of service themselves became mere steps or stages on the way to priesthood. The higher orders had positions such as bishops, and eventually even higher orders such as archbishops (Metropolitans in the Eastern Church), Cardinals and Popes were all on the scene.

Most traditional Churches have considered their modes of order as being required or at least paradigmatic. Churches in the Catholic tradition (Anglican, Orthodox, and Roman Catholic) have made one of the marks of the Church that it is apostolic, meaning by this that it can trace its origins through a line of Bishops to the apostles themselves, the so called apostolic succession as we saw.

The "free churches" (Presbyterians, Methodists, Baptists, etc.) do not accept this notion. For one thing it is not found in the Bible and did not appear until some time after the apostolic age. If it is so essential one would think it should have been more clearly laid down by Jesus himself or at least by the earliest apostolic writers.[8]

What seems to be the obvious interpretation of the New Testament teaching about the Church it that the important question is not how it should be organized but what it is, the body of Christ. The particular organizational forms that the Church should adopt are those which are suitable to the times in which we live and the work that we have to do.

---

[7] The term *laicos* was originally an honorific title meaning one of the people of God, not an amateur as it tended to become.

[8] The treatment of church order here is essentially that found in *The Church, the Churches, and the Sacraments* by the great Methodist theologian of a former generation J. Agar Beet. (London: Hodder and Stoughton, 1907).

The early church managed with very little in the form of structures of ministry and seemed mainly concerned with members exercising the gifts that they had been given. Most churches, like the Jewish congregations before them, quickly came to the conclusion that preachers and teachers were very important and required careful selection and special training. The ultimate supervision of the preachers, and the church generally, is now performed by an annual Conference of some kind or other. In the interim between annual conclaves, supervision of church affairs is carried out by subsidiary bodies (Synods, Presbyteries and the like) with officers who superintend the day to day activities of the Church. In the free churches these officers operate more or less like bishops. Indeed American Methodism, in addition to district superintendents, has adopted bishops to superintend the activity of an entire conference area.[9]

So it would seem that the New Testament has nothing more to tell us about orders of ministry except that they are not inscribed in tablets of stone. But there is much more to be said. The problem with all types of church ministerial orders is still the problem of the laity, who tend in each pattern to be passive receivers of the ministries of the official orders. And this has become recognized by most if not all churches as a great error: the entire membership of the church are in fact ministers. Pope Francis spoke to this end while addressing Catholics in Brazil. When someone came and told Moses that others were prophesying and that they had silenced them, Moses, great man that he was, said "Would God that all the Lord's people were prophets and that he would put his spirit into them," (Numbers 11:29). And we are not like tools or pieces of machinery with just one function. The gifts mentioned in St. Paul's letter to the Ephesians were not allotted one at a time to individual Christians. Each of us has many gifts. Moses would tell us that we are all expected to be prophets, listening to God and passing on what he tells us in various ways, spoken and unspoken. Likewise we are all pastors caring for the sheep, and evangelists spreading the Kingdom of God. We are

---

[9] American bishops are elected for life by jurisdictions composed of several conferences. They are not elected by the conferences in which they will serve, and move around from one conference to another after a period of years.

even apostles, sent by God as missionaries to a needy world. Of course we each are likely to be somewhat specialized, having one or more gifts in a greater degree than others, but we are expected to use all of them. God has given them to us and will help us to use them. The parable of the talents (Luke 19:12–28) would also tell us that when we exercise the gifts that come to hand, we will find that we have others as well.[10] The best way to find God's will for our lives is to ask what he wants us to do today. The future will then begin to open up, new gifts emerging as we use those that we already have.

On Worship

The earliest forms of worship in ancient Israel are matters for historical scholarship and are necessarily speculative, but likely involved music, probably chanting, perhaps dancing and the reading of the law. With the establishment of worship in the tabernacle in David's time, and later in Solomon's temple, there were large organized corps of musicians who played instruments and both composed and sang psalms. Presumably the law was read and commentary provided.

With the supplementation or replacement of temple worship with services in the synagogues we have more information.[11] The building was plain and rectangular, with benches for the elders at the front, and a reading desk and an arc or box which contained the rolls of the scriptures. The congregation had a ruler or chairman who presided. With Hasidic Jews there was singing, generally of a rather lively character. The rolls of the law were brought out and paraded round before being read. There was normally one reading from the law and another from the prophets. Any adult Jew could be asked to read the scriptures and a visitor might be asked to comment on the reading and perhaps give a word of encouragement to the congregation. Jesus

---

[10] The Lord said to the profitable servants, "Well done—you have been faithful in few things, I will put you in charge of many things." Matt 25:24–30.

[11] If there was no synagogue in a gentile city, the devout would meet near a river, St. Paul met Lydia, a wealthy business woman and a God fearer near Thyatira in this manner. She became the first convert in Europe and St. Paul and his companions stayed at her house (Acts 14).

and later St. Paul functioned as visiting readers and speakers in this way. There would also be formal prayers beginning with the preface to the Ten Commandments, the *Shema* (Hear, O Israel). Set prayers would be read and each one was followed by the congregation saying "Amen" (may it be so), a custom that has been continued in Christian worship. The lively instrumental music of the temple was forbidden in the synagogues by the rabbis and replaced by chanting, often antiphonal.

The earliest Christian meetings took place in the temple courts but soon, and especially when the church spread beyond Jerusalem, they would meet in the house of some Christian person or in a gentile lecture hall that was not in use at that time.[12] If there was no synagogue the congregation customarily met beside a river. (Acts 16) We know from the Epistle of James that at least some Jewish Christians followed the synagogue format in their worship.[13]

At first it was common for Christian congregations to meet in the Jewish synagogues. But there seems to have been a growing antipathy to Christians on the part of non-Christian Jews and this practice was discontinued. Christian services were then held on Sunday, the Lord's Day, which was the first day of creation and also the day of the Resurrection.[14] In the synagogues women were not permitted to join in the singing, at least for some time, but in the Christian services men and women both joined in the singing, which was apparently often antiphonal in character with one group of singers leading and another responding. And the singing may not have been confined to chanting, for St. Paul exhorts the Christians to sing and make melody in your hearts with psalms and hymns and spiritual songs (Eph 5:19). Also some quotations in the New Testament epistles[15] sound like the verses of a Christian hymn.

---

[12] St. Paul taught and presumably worshipped in the lecture room of the philosopher Tyrannus in Ephesus for two years (Acts 17). The Christian community may have worshipped there or in some such place on occasion.

[13] See James 2 where the ruler asks a wealthy person to take an honored seat and a poor man to sit on the floor.

[14] See the first apology of Justin Martyr circa AD 150.

[15] For example, "Awake thou that steepest and Christ shall give thee light."

The service of Holy Communion was at first held every Lord's day and was preceded by a love feast. Wealthier Christians brought food and distributed it to all present.[16] The love feast was then followed by the service of Holy Communion. Abuses in the love feast, such as those mentioned by St. Paul (1 Cor 11) where the wealthier feasted and drank and the poor had nothing to eat, may have led to the demise of the love feast, and the communion service proceeded on its own. John Wesley of course revived the love feast as a sort of communion service where there was no ordained minister to officiate at the sacrament. The members would have bread and water and share testimony as to what the Lord had done for them since their last meeting. Love feasts continued to be held in Ireland until recent times.[17]

Worship in the reformed churches featured the usual mix of the reading of scripture, singing, prayer and preaching. In the stricter Presbyterian services only the psalms were used in singing as it was thought that there was no language fit for the worship of God except what God had provided in the Scriptures. In the Church of England the psalms were chanted in plain song. Among the Presbyterians the psalms were rendered (sometimes tortured) into metrical form and sung to secular tunes. Among the earlier and stricter Presbyterians it was also considered wrong to sing the sacred words outside the worship service and so often silly words were provided for use in choir practice during the week. There was also among Presbyterians, for a considerable time, objection to instrumental music, especially the introduction of the organ into worship. Hymns, other than paraphrases of scripture, were also prohibited for a time. The Methodist revival of course featured hymns set to catchy tunes and they, together with instrumental music of various kinds, have become an important part of worship.

The reading of scripture in worship merits some attention. It was of course of prime importance in the synagogue services and

---

[16] St. Augustine noted with approval how his mother Monica brought extra food to the love feast for poor persons

[17] Rev. Austin Hassard describes them as they still existed in his boyhood in Fermanagh, where the leader prayed every week "Lord soak our souls in grace like a fum turf in a bog hole".

also in established Christian worship right through the Middle Ages, especially since the greater part of the congregation would be unable to read the Bible for themselves. With the invention of printing, Bibles became available both to smaller churches and individual persons, but still the reading of the scriptures remained an important part of public worship. The readings from the Bible were therefore extensive and commonly included fairly lengthy excerpts from the Old Testament, the Psalms, the Gospels, and then the Epistles. As the importance of preaching became emphasized (and required more time) readings from the scriptures tended to become fewer and shorter. This has been generally perceived to be undesirable and the tendency is now to have more extensive Bible readings. The manner of reading has also begun to be more appreciated. In former times the main qualification to be a reader was just to be able to read. It has become appreciated more recently that to read the scriptures in worship one should be able to read well. The effective reading of scripture in divine worship can and should be a very important part of the service. Training of readers, ministers and lay persons alike, to read clearly and effectively has become recognized to be most important.

 A recent development has been the introduction of what are termed *praise songs*. These are really simple hymns with repeated expressions of praise to God put to modern styles of tune. They have been popular with young people and are often accompanied with clapping of the hands and other expressions of joy. Older Christians are concerned about the dubious poetic quality of many of these hymns and also consider the accompanying hand clapping undignified, terming them as "happy-clappy" numbers. Whether praise songs are here to stay remains to be seen, but they are here, and churches and congregations must decide what to do with them. Some ban them altogether and some blend the two styles together. A third approach, now very common, is to have two services, one traditional and the other a praise service. Sunday school is often located in between the two services so that those leaving the early service and those going to the later one can join together in Sunday school.[18]

Perhaps the most important point to note is that the forms and even the content of worship is less important than the manner in which it is carried out. Jesus wished the worship of God to be "in spirit and in truth" (John chapter 4), which means that it is to be whole hearted and directed to the One who is present with us as promised.

SUGGESTIONS FOR FURTHER READING

Flew's *Jesus and His Church* is crucial reading here (and it is also listed among the suggested readings for chapter four).

Beet, Joseph Agar. *The Church, the Churches, and the Sacraments*. London: Hodder and Stoughton, 1907. Print. Biblical theology presented here by a nineteenth century master.

Clowney, Edmund P. *The Doctrine of the Church*. Philadelphia: Presbyterian and Reformed Pub., 1969. Print.

Hildebrandt, Franz. *From Luther to Wesley*. London: Lutterworth, 1951. Print.

Mark Dever's "An Introduction to the Church", is available online at the Theology Network.

Worrall, Stanley. *Who Are We?: What Do We Believe?* Belfast: Christian Journals, 1977. Print. This is a most valuable little book with presentations by scholarly representatives of the various churches in Ireland. It has obvious value outside of Ireland too.

---

[18] In Britain Sunday School is only provided for children and perhaps young folks. In America it is usual to continue Sunday school from cradle to the grave.

VIII

Thinking about the Sacraments

The term *sacramentum* was quite commonly taken by preachers of a former generation to mean the soldier's oath which he took on entering the Roman army. But more properly, in connection with baptism and the Lord's Supper, it is a translation of the Greek term *mysterion* (mystery), which in New Testament times commonly referred to the rituals used in religious cults.[1] The meaning of these rituals was only clear to members of the cult. This makes more sense in explaining the sacraments of the Christian Church. They are ritual acts with a hidden meaning. The Roman Catholic Church acknowledges seven sacraments. The scriptures only mention two, those of baptism and the Lord's Supper. It is true that there are many significant rituals referenced, marriage being one, but baptism and the Lord's Supper were enjoined by the Lord and so are called the *dominical* sacraments.

The Lord's Supper

The Lord's Supper was initiated in the upper room where Jesus met with the twelve apostles to celebrate the Passover together. The Passover ritual indeed dominates the interpretation of the Lord's Supper. The Passover meal, or *Seder*, is an ancient Jewish ritual celebrating the delivery of God's people from slavery in Egypt and it is described as a memorial. The term memorial (*anamnesis* in Greek and *Zikaron* in Hebrew) is only very weakly translated as a reminder. It was not designed merely to remind the Israelites of the greatest event in their history, but to reenact it. Every item and every action in the rite is a rerun of the Exodus. Bitter herbs represent their bondage in Egypt; salt water represents the sea that they crossed; unleavened bread was used as the Israelites had to prepare their rations for the journey in haste;

---

[1] For instance the cult of Mithras, which was popular with Roman soldiers.

the lamb shank represents the sacrifice offered to God, with the blood sprinkled on the door posts, on the eve of their departure. The meal is even taken in the reclining position representing that they are no longer slaves but free.

Jesus reinterpreted the Passover meal, as he did the law and everything else, and he clearly took it to represent the greater deliverance that he was initiating for all mankind. The elements are the bread and the wine. Jesus said "This is my body broken for you," and, "this is my blood shed for you. Whenever you eat this bread and drink this cup, do so as a memorial of me." Non Catholics note that he can hardly have been meaning his physical body which was there in the room with them. But the difference between evangelicals and Catholics is not as great as it might seem. Lutherans, Calvinists and the Wesley's all believed in the real presence of Jesus in the sacrament in a special sense. For just as the Israelites reenacted the great deliverance of the Exodus, we reenact the greater deliverance wrought by Jesus in the New Testament. Interpreting the meaning of the rite depends on how you see or define the term "body". In the New Testament the body is not just seen as flesh, but as the means by which we operate in our environment. St. Paul said there is one body for the seed as it lives in the ground and another for the flower when it emerges into the sunlight and air. So there is one body for us in this life and a different one for our life after death (1 Cor 15:38). Jesus had an ordinary body during his incarnation but his resurrected form was reportedly heightened or different.[2]

What is the meaning of the rite? The actual bread and wine are perhaps not the most important. The ancients said *non signum sed signatum*.[3] It is what they represent that is important. As we take the bread into our bodies we are receiving the Risen Jesus into our lives, and as we drink the wine we are appropriating to ourselves the benefits of the sacrifice that He has made on our behalf. Eating and drinking is, of course, a regular event in our daily lives, but it is made real to us in a special way by the *dominical* rite. It enacts, what words could never fully express,

---

[2] An intermediate and third kind of body may be implied in the resurrection appearances where Jesus actually ate with the disciples.

[3] Not the sign but what it signifies.

the central matter of the Gospel, taught all over the New Testament, that Christ enters into our hearts and dwells there and that this is God's salvation. It is also a proclamation.[4] We proclaim Christ's saving death in a real way. And finally it is a feast, it celebrates our salvation and it looks forward to the greater feast, the heavenly banquet in the Kingdom of God.[5]

Baptism

Baptism was a regular ritual among the Jews in Jesus' time. If heathens converted, they enacted or expressed this great change by a ceremonial washing and a complete change of clothes, putting off the filth of heathendom and beginning a new life as a member of God's family Israel. This was described by them as being born all over again. Nicodemus could not understand what Jesus was talking about when He told him (John 3) that he had to be born again, for he was already an Israelite and did not need to be born twice. But Jesus told him that He was talking about spiritual things; not just becoming an Israelite in body but entering the Kingdom of God. John the Baptist told the Jews the same thing. He said that they should have no confidence in the fact that they were the descendants of Abraham, for God could raise up children to Abraham out of the stones lying around them in the desert. It was not enough to be by nature an Israelite, it was necessary to be spiritually one of God's family. John's insistence that the Jews needed to be baptized was telling them that they were virtually heathen and had to be made ready for the coming of the Messiah by being baptized as if they were coming new into God's family.

Jesus and His disciples carried on the tradition of baptism, signifying entry into the new Israel, the body of Christ. Obviously this would initially be of adult persons who heard and responded to the gospel and wished to become a member of the Christian Church. The question of what happened to their families is less easy to answer. We cannot go back into the early church to a time when baptism of the family did not include the children. The

---

[4] "...for in so doing we proclaim the Lord's death till be comes." 1 Cor 11:

[5] "I will drink no more of the fruit of the vine till I drink it new in the Kingdom of God." Mark 14:25.

practice of baptizing only adults was not an option because they wanted their children to be part of the new Israel, to be children of the promise. The Baptist tradition, believer's baptism, is a relatively modern arrival.

So when those in the *paedobaptist* tradition, baptize infants they are celebrating their entry into the family of the Church, to be raised in that family with and for God. Baptism is described in Col 2:11–12 as being like circumcision. Gentiles were circumcised on becoming Jews and so were their children. The children of Jews were circumcised when they were only a few days old, signifying that they were then in the family of God. But as they approached adult life, they had to choose whether they would accept this for themselves or not. This is the ceremony of *bar-mitzvah*, for a son of the Covenant, or *bet'-mitzvah* which is the equivalent for modern Jewish girls. We can apply this understanding to the practice of paedo-baptism (the baptizing of children). The parents choose for them to be brought up in the Christian family and later they must decide whether to accept this act done on their behalf or not. The Methodist Church, for example, recognizes members and adherents, just as the Jews distinguished between Jews proper and the "God fearers", those who frequented the Jewish community but were not circumcised and did not keep the Jewish law as to foods etc. Baptized children are not merely adherents but, like the children of Jews, members of the community who are not yet able or obliged to choose for themselves whether they will be full members or not. So all *paedobaptist* churches (Roman Catholic, Anglican, Orthodox, Presbyterian and Methodist) have a ceremony, generally preceded by a series of classes, where the young elect for themselves to belong to the body of Christ. This goes under different names in different churches, confirmation is one, and may lead up to taking communion for the first time, though the ordering differs greatly.

And what of our Baptist friends, are they so very different? The meaning and practice of baptism is not the same as with most other churches, but the understanding of the Church and church membership is not really different from the *paedobaptist* tradition. The children are not outsiders till baptized, but are brought into the church by their parents and dedicated to God, just as Hannah gave the infant Samuel back to God (1 Sam 1) and are treated as children of the promise.

Let us return next, and look more carefully at one of the issues raised by this discussion.

The Real Presence in the Eucharist

Transubstantiation is the official position of the Roman Catholic Church on the nature of the elements in the Eucharist. It is stated in terms of medieval philosophy (with Aristotelian roots) where everything has a *substance*, which is a "things" true *nature*, and a substance is something that always remains the same. This *substance* is distinguished from the *accidents* or properties of the thing, which can and do vary. So a horse has a substance which does not alter, but also accidents, such as size and color and other qualities, which vary from horse to horse, and even vary with the same horse over time.[6] Seen from within this sort of system or framework, the bread and wine of the Eucharist retain their accidental qualities, color, and taste, etc., but their substance has changed into the flesh and blood of Christ.

With the related *consubstantiation*, the bread and wine remain what they are but the body and blood of Christi is delivered with them (*con* being the Latin *cum*, meaning with). This was the view of the medieval philosopher John Duns Scotus.[7] It is held by some Lutherans and some Anglicans.

Sacramental Union insists that when Christ said "This is my body...", his words forever united his body with the bread and wine which are then received by all communicants whether they are believers or not. This is the official position of Lutherans and is often supplemented with other views.

The *Eucharist* can also be treated as a mystery. Here, the real presence of the body and blood of Christ in the Eucharist is asserted but with no precise details as to the means involved, and

---

[6] Linguistic philosophers trace this view back to the distinction between, and confusion concerning, the functions of nouns and adjectives.

[7] An influential philosopher and theologian in the High Middle Ages (1266–1308), known as the subtle doctor. A statue representing him has been erected in Berwick, Scotland ; he was canonized in 1993.

hence the mystery. This is generally the view of the Orthodox churches, with a meaning that approaches much the same thing as the Roman Catholic Church, but omitting the notion of transubstantiation, preferring a reverent silence as to an explanation of the matter.

Pneumatic presence, is the view of some reformed theologians. By this is meant a real spiritual presence, where the spirit of Jesus is imparted to believers by the power of the Spirit. The remaining question not dealt with here is how this relates to the true body and blood of Jesus.

It is important to note what is common to all of these approaches that being that all these affirm the **real presence** of Christ in the Eucharist.

Other churches employ a different understanding of the term "memorial." The Swiss radical reformer Zwingli accepted the weak sense of memorial as meaning a reminder only. A number of Protestant denominations take this view including most Baptists.

The Methodist understanding of the Lord's Supper explicitly rejects transubstantiation but affirms a real presence of Christ in the rite. It is interesting that in the Methodist Book of Offices the rite is described as a *reenactment* of Christ's suffering and death, and not merely a reminder.

At issue through all this, is what we mean by the *body and blood* of Jesus. If the actual physical body of Jesus from while he was on earth is intended, it is indeed a strange notion which a number of Catholic theologians are quick to disavow by distinguishing the real presence from cannibalism. If on the other hand, it refers to the heavenly body of Jesus, the concept of the real presence in the Eucharist should not be objectionable to evangelicals as it is what we believe is the nature of salvation and which is taught everywhere in the New Testament. All that is needed perhaps on the part of the recipient is the humble intention to receive the Risen Christ into one's innermost being.

SUGGESTIONS FOR FURTHER READING

The relevant chapters of Flew's *Jesus and His Church* are again indispensable here, and the relevant parts of *The Book of Common Prayer* are also worth reading,

> Wood, James, and Church of England. *The Book of Common Prayer (and Administration of the Sacraments and Other Rites and Ceremonies of the Church According to the Use of the Church of England...)* New York, NY: Penguin, 2012. Print.

Wikipedia's articles on "The Eucharist" and "The Real Presence in the Eucharist" are both useful, the latter in large part due to its discussion of the variety of views on this subject held by various Christian denominations.

The Catholic Encyclopedia Online similarly has a good article on "The Eucharist."

IX

Thinking about Worship

People describe attending worship in different ways. In Andy Griffith's TV show, set in the rural town of Mayberry, it is referred to as "going to preaching". In the mountains of North Carolina it may be termed as heading off to "praise the Lord' where the emphasis will be on the music and singing. People likewise differ in what they consider a good service, or in the reasons they give for attending one church rather than another (perhaps this one has a good preacher while another a friendly congregation). And perhaps all of these reasons miss the mark. Christian worship is meeting with the Lord and acknowledging his worth. The term worship means "worth-ship". It was used of a formal meeting of the notables of the realm with the King, and in that way acknowledging his worth, who he was, and his right to their service. Divine Service mean something similar. We are gathered to meet with our Maker, to acknowledge his greatness and offer Him all that we are and have. All through the Bible, worship is centered round the presence of God, who is there by promise. As the communion hymn puts it, "I come with joy to meet my Lord." Reportedly, and this was a while back, someone phoned the rector of the Church at Balmoral, where the Royal family worshipped, and asked if the King would be present at the service that day. The rector replied, "I cannot tell, but the King of Kings will certainly be present". And he was spot on with this remark.

Every part of divine service should reflect its overall purpose then. We begin with an invocation (said, sung, prayed or however) which is nothing else other than asking God to be present and meet with us as promised.

Singing Hymns

Hymns and music are traditionally a very important part of the service among most denominations. But what are we doing when we sing? Properly speaking we are singing to God, praising and thanking Him, as well as offering Him our service and love, and so it should be done in a whole hearted manner. Mr. Wesley's recommendation to the singers we saw earlier, was to "sing heartily and in time," (and certainly in tune too, if that is amongst our gifts). If we have not sung heartily to God, on this view, we have not worshipped properly. St. Paul exhorted his Ephesian church members not to be drunk with wine (no drunken bellowing) but to join together, "with psalms and hymns and spiritual songs, singing and making merry unto the Lord in your hearts (Eph 5:9). Many of us remember our parents and elders singing hymns as they worked or while they relaxed in the evenings. And it was a happy sound. We are blessed with a great tradition of hymnody, not only in Charles Wesley and Isaac Watts (top of the charts now for several centuries), but with many other great hymn writers and musicians since. Wesley said that a good hymn was poetry set to good music. A great hymn writer therefore is not just someone who can arrange words in rhythm and rhyme. Real poets have a certain fire about them, and this can be said of the great hymn writers of every generation. They did not simply sing, rather, they burst into song. The writer of John's apocalypse periodically could not contain himself it seems and burst forth onto the page with great paeans of praise. These majestic eruptions have been the inspiration of many hymn writers and musicians ever since, with Handel's *Messiah* surely to be counted among the greatest of these.

Scripture

The reading and explanation of Scripture has always been a vital part of worship services. This was especially the case when few people could read and even fewer possessed a Bible, but it is still very much the case today. The reading of scripture should not be treated as the preliminary to the sermon. It is God speaking to us after all, and should be treated as such. Scripture readings have been reduced both in number and length since the time of my youth. In the church I grew up in, we had three readings (often accompanied with a comment): one from the Old Testament (sometimes with a psalm thrown in for good measure); one from a gospel; and one from the epistles or some other of the New Testament text. The importance of the reading of the scriptures in a service has traditionally been emphasized in a formal way. In the Jewish synagogue where it was the central part or worship, it was preceded by bringing the parchment roll out of the arc and parading it round the sanctuary. The Scottish Kirk had the same idea, carrying the Bible into the pulpit and setting it down to show its central place in worship. Episcopal churches often also parade a copy of a Gospel round the church before reading it. And other churches use special words in introducing the reading of the Bible, some declaring, "Let us hear the Word of God as we find it," and ending with a similar solemn formula. All this is goes to emphasize that we are not just listening to someone reading a good book, but seeking to hear God Himself speaking to us when it is read aloud. God speaks to us all the time no doubt, but nowhere more clearly than when we are hearing his Word from the Bible, and especially when we hear it together in worship.

The manner of the reading then is clearly also very important, so allow me to repeat an earlier point here, by briefly taking to the pulpit. The Bible should be *well* read in worship, not mumbled or hurried. We should more earnestly train our young ministers to read as well as to preach, and similarly instruct our young people and lay readers in much the same way. It is a hard lesson to learn that reading in public is different from simply talking. It is best done slowly and distinctly and with genuine concern for the meaning of the text. We should also listen expectantly when the Bible is being read in worship. Attentive or active listening should be followed by responding to what God is saying to us. The Bible read clearly and intelligently in the Church service to a listening people is a most powerful part of worship.

Prayer
Permit me, if you will, to occupy the pulpit a moment longer.

Prayer and prayers are an important feature in the Church service and here again it bears remembering just what we are doing when we engage in public prayer. The description once given of a prayer as being the finest ever offered to a Boston audience was intended as a compliment, but phrased as such it was a condemnation. We should keep in mind that in prayer we are praying to God and in a service we are doing it together.

Conducting prayer in church has been correctly described as *leading* in prayer, though unfortunately leaders are often on their own with few if any of us following. Here again I believe we can better instruct our young ministers, and indeed anyone else who may be leading a service of worship, by helping them to conduct public prayer meaningfully. It is certainly worthwhile keeping in mind that there are various sorts of prayer that play a part in worship in this regard.

The prayer of *humble access* brings us before God in confessing our sins, and snippets of scripture are often included as part of this to be helpful reminders of the One to whom we praying in hope of His mercy. This is closely related to, and followed by, thanksgiving.

Intercessory prayer is quite a separate matter. It is based on Jesus saying to us that to ask is to receive; that to seek is to find. Note too, that we are not told exactly what we will receive nor precisely the hour when, but we are instructed to ask in faith. James warns us that if we are in two minds about what we are asking for we receive nothing (James 1:7). It is important, without doubt, to always encourage a congregation to actively participate in prayers of intercession. In many Korean churches when the minister says "let us pray," everybody starts praying their own prayers out loud. It is noisy but at the very least everyone is participating. Another useful way of encouraging congregational participation in the prayers is to suggest topics, or special concerns or even specific people, and then pause between each item to allow the congregation to pray for that concern themselves in the silence.

I cannot leave this topic and platform without lastly encouraging members to join in the prayer with an "Amen". This was perhaps overdone in times past when it became something of a formal ritual. But, I think that it is now sadly underdone. A meaningful and heartfelt congregational "Amen" at an appropriate point in a prayer is very helpful to fellow worshippers as well as to the one conducting prayer, for it indicates active involvement of the congregation in the prayers.

All told, I think that church members should be encouraged to pray more; to believe in prayer as a ministry given by God to us all, and to meet for prayer together during the week. Dr. Billy Kim (the Billy Graham of Asia) has commented more than once that if he had his life to live over again, he would preach less and pray more.

Preaching the Sermon

The sermon is given central importance and pride of place in protestant churches but its true nature is often missed. It was earlier noted and is indeed noteworthy that in the lists of church offices in the New Testament there is no mention of preachers; teachers and pastors are there of course, but not preachers explicitly. This is, I suspect, just a matter of the name, for in the New Testament preachers are described as prophets, those people called by God to listen to Him and to then pass on what He tells them to others. And this is what preaching is or should aspire to be. The Holy Spirit provides the message or in fact lights up the one the preacher already has in mind. We after all ordain our preachers but we do not call them, since that is done by God, just as He called Isaiah and Jeremiah. And it is interesting to note that there need be no male preference here. Phillip we're told had four daughters all prophetesses (as we see in Acts 4:19). What a household! And so we should extend the call to prophesy to all Christians. Moses, we noted earlier, wished that all the Lord's people were prophets, all listening to God and proclaiming God's message, each in our own way. Recalling also that the sermon is not a spectator sport we might do well to remember that we are not only listening *to* the sermon but *through* the sermon.

The Collection

The offering was referred to in the church of my youth as the collection, but it is much more. Our gifts are a grateful return to

God of what He has given us and the gift in money represents the gift of ourselves and all that we have and are. Little children can understand this very well and an offering well explained can be a very important part of a children's Sunday school class or a children's meeting. I well remember how we sang in the infants Sunday school class, "See the pennies dropping, hear the pennies fall, every one for Jesus, He will have them all." One of the attendees of that class became Dr. Maureen Turtle, later a missionary doctor in Burma. She brought her entire pocket money every week for those less fortunate. The offering has lost some of its significance with the advent of organized giving to the Church, where once a month an envelope with a check is deposited in the offering plate. This is good for church administration but it is less personal. One practice that is helpful here is to lay one's hand on the plate or other receptacle, even when giving nothing, and offer ourselves before passing it on to the next person.

The Blessing

The final event in the service is the blessing or benediction. This does not just mark the conclusion of the service, it can be the pinnacle or high point (some leave the offering to this point for the same purpose). But whether it is pronounced by the ministrant or by the congregation acting together, it should be seen as a real event; asking God to do what he always wishes to do, send us out from His presence with His blessing.

These are just some points that have occurred to me over the years as I have been attending worship services. If you attend a service to enjoy the music, or to hear an interesting of even an inspiring address, or, worse, to meet your friends, you will eventually, or maybe sooner, be disappointed. But if you go to meet the Lord; to worship Him as you sing, to join with others in prayer, and to listen for his voice in every part of the service, you will never come away without feeling that in one way or another you have been blessed. And if you are really listening for God's Word for you in the sermon, you will never hear a bad sermon. Promise.

SUGGESTIONS FOR FURTHER READING

Packer, J. I. *Knowing God*. Downers Grove, IL: InterVarsity, 1973. Print.

MacDonald, Gordon. *Who Stole My Church?: What to Do When the Church You Love Tries to Enter the Twenty-first Century*. Nashville, TN: Thomas Nelson, 2007. Print.

The books of worship and offices used by various denominations contain beautiful prayers and invaluable resources. As a result they are well worth reviewing and rereading. Most of those in English are based on medieval prayer books and closely resemble one another.

The article on "Christian Worship" on Wikipedia has good information on worship services as they vary between denominations. The more extensive and wide ranging article there on "Worship Services" is also useful, containing valuable information on many types of worship, Christian and non-Christian alike.

X
Thinking about the Christian Life

When people become Christians, their most obvious question can be, "What next?", because the right way forward is not always clear to them. Evangelists who check into the matter find that new converts frequently flounder and fall away and that the relapse rate is uncomfortably high. Estimates that approach a 90% failure rate have been reported following very successful and well-designed evangelistic crusades. Serious evangelists know that everything depends on the follow up and try to connect the new converts to active churches who will nurture and support them. This is much needed, for they are like newborn babes coming into the world in a hostile environment. Two important questions face the new Christian namely, Where do I go from here?, and, How should I go about getting there? The New Testament writers answer this question invariably by urging the new Christians to "grow in grace and in the knowledge of our Lord and Savior Jesus Christ." (1 Pet 3:18) They describe new converts as newborn babies who need to be cared for, nourished and exercised. John Wesley's famous sermon on the new birth says that those who are newly born again need to breathe, feed and exercise. He also speaks of this process as availing ourselves of the means of Grace. What though, are these means of grace and how should we go about availing ourselves of them? The means of grace are five in number: namely prayer, worship, fellowship, studying the scriptures, and Christian work, and I'll tackle each of these in what follows.

Prayer

John Wesley compares prayer to breathing; breathing in the Spirit of God and pouring it out again in thanksgiving, praise and love. This makes for a beautiful description of prayer. Brother Lawrence described this as *the practice of the presence of God*; and he found it in his daily life as well as his devotions.[1] Our prayers often consist largely of petitions, asking for this, that and the other, and there is nothing wrong with this. Prayer is just learning to talk with God (not just talking to Him) and our daily concerns are important to God. In fact we get to know God in sharing our concerns with him as well just enjoying His presence. And it is our duty, as the *Book of Common Prayer* tells us to pray for all sorts of people and whatever might befall them. Praying, of whatever sort, is part of living in God's company. When you live with anyone, you get to know them and communicate back and forward with them at many levels. This binds people together. The most profound example of this is marriage where two people become one (Gen 2:21–24). There are many books written on how to pray, but the best way is just to start talking with and listening to God: in short, praying and living in the presence of God. To pray in this way is to get to know God and to mature as Christians.

Worship

Regular worship is very important. The old comment that we are not saved by attending church is true, but only a half truth. We are unlikely to progress in the faith and grow in grace without regular church attendance. John Wesley, when inclined to overmuch solitary devotion, was told that the Bible knows nothing of solitary religion. This was wise advice. It is true that God is with us at all times, but He is with us in a special way when we gather to worship. God is social and the Christian life including worship is inescapably social. Christ's promise is that when two or three are gathered together in His name, He is there in their midst. Church services vary in appeal and some seem to benefit us and others not. But if we go to meet God and listen for His voice in the various parts of the service we are very unlikely to leave the church feeling that God was not there. It might be good here to reread the chapters on Worship and the Sacraments.

---

[1] Lawrence. *The Practice of the Presence of God.* (2012)

Fellowship

The company and fellowship of our fellow Christians is an important means of grace. The old adage "show me your company and I'll tell you what you are," runs true both for good and ill. Wesley was told that he must either find Christian companions or make them. The military know the importance of fellowship all too well. Soldiers do not undertake acts of extreme bravery, as they often do, for their country alone but as much for their comrades, and therefore forging group loyalty is an important part of military training. Clinical psychologists know the same thing and use it in group therapy. A person with mental disorders will fare much better if they have strong family links or good friends. Alcoholic rehabilitation, including Alcoholics Anonymous, makes great use of the same principle, forging and strengthening links between the members of the group. The same principle holds for those who travel to heaven. The road is hard and we gain much strength and comfort as we travel it together. The Church must form strong bonds among its members. Mr. Wesley, wise man, quickly learned this lesson and formed his Methodists into classes which met weekly to share their joys or sorrows, or burdens of any kind, and to pray for one another. The same advice that was given to John Wesley holds for us. If you cannot find good companions you must make them. Create or join a fellowship group and cultivate Christian friends.

The Study of the Bible

We must also grow in the knowledge of God and of His Son Jesus Christ, and this brings us to the study of the Bible. An understanding of God's Word does not arrive with us on the day of our conversion to God. Like prayer, it has to be developed. It is not just learning off passages of scripture by rote, though I am very glad that I was encouraged to do this early in life. Instead, we must do more, which means we must ponder and think about what we read and let the words and phrases become part of us. Moses commanded the Israelites to bind the commandments on their foreheads and onto their forearms, these two representing thought and work.² (Deut 6:6–8) We should carefully reflect on what we read and allow it to be built into the fabric of our being, not just tasting but chewing and thereby incorporating the Word of God into the deepest recesses off our minds and hearts. Incorporating the scriptures into our thinking and living in this way is what the Bible describes as becoming wise. The least educated person who comes to know and love the Bible becomes wise. They have graduated in the greatest school of all.

Exercise

Work too is terribly important, as a means of grace. Babies begin exercising their limbs (and their voices) as soon as they are born, and so must the Christian. Work is in fact a particularly important means of grace. Wesley noted that love must flow outward in practical ways. The Dead Sea is dead after all because it has no outlet. A Christian that has not experienced the joy of Christian work has missed a lot and lost plenty. Wesley advised his members, "never to be unemployed and never to be triflingly employed." There are several ways in which we should be busy.

First, we need to be busy in the work of the church. A church cannot be properly run with the paid professionals doing all the work. A functioning church needs an army of workers. The administration alone is no small matter. Visiting those from the congregation in hospital or retirement homes or just at home is not simply a matter for the ministers, it is everyone's ministry. Evangelism is likewise everyone's job. Some of the best evangelism is carried out by ordinary church members who simply invite others to church or to meetings of some kind. Garrison Keillor, of "Prairie Home Companion" fame, had a very religious upbringing but got away from it for a number of reasons, including his busy professional life. Many people in fact asked him why he did not attend church, and eventually someone invited him to come to church with them and he went and continued going ever since. I visited Campbell University's sister law school in South Korea a few years ago and was impressed by the custom that the

---

[2] The shroud of Turin shows a phylactery on the forehead and one on the forearm.

students had of singing a hymn and praying before every class. Coming up out of the subway I observed young people handing out pamphlets to all who passed by. I thought they were Jehovah's witnesses or some such; but they were just the young people of a local church using their lunch hour to invite everyone to join them at worship. I purchased some necklaces in a Korean jewelry store for my grandnieces and as the purchase was completed the lovely young sales lady smiled at me and said a few words in Korean. I asked the Korean Law professor with me what she was saying and he told me that she was inviting me to her Church. I couldn't help but be impressed.

Second, Christian work does not end at the church door but goes out with us into our daily occupations, whatever they may be. There is a difference, often hard to define, in the way a Christian goes about their ordinary work. You can begin to suspect that someone is Christian just by the way they do their tasks and treat people. The Campbell University Doctor of Pharmacy School has a strong Christian fellowship. I once attended one of their group meetings and asked them why they chose to become pharmacists. Uniformly they told me it was to help people. I was initially puzzled at this answer until I began to notice how they treated the elderly customers who formed a large part of their clientele. These senior citizens often had very little idea of what their drugs were intended for, or how to take them. They had been told something perfunctorily in the doctor's office no doubt, but it hadn't registered with them. The time and patience shown to these elderly people by the Christian pharmacists was a ministry in itself, and I am sure that it greatly improved their patient's treatments and outlooks. When I see this kind of attitude in any kind of professional person, I ask them as an opener if they go to church and inevitably this kind of person says "Yes." Without saying a word, they have been saying a great deal; and if ever the topic of Church or manner of living comes round, any little word they may say will carry a lot of weight. It is also worth saying here that it is a great help, if one "carries the flag", that is wearing some badge or piece of jewelry that identifies you as a Christian (some choose a tattoo). This may encourage someone, especially one who has taken note of your manner of life, to ask you why you wear it.

Third, our competence in our profession or job is very important. A Christian is called to be as good at their work as they can be. Even students have this obligation. They do not have to be at the top of the class, but they should be at the place where interest and conscientious study will take them. Our founding Dean in the Campbell University Law School, Leary Davis, said that a high place in class ranking was not a reliable mark of a future good lawyer. A better indicator of the future was how they went about preparing for their future career, being well prepared for class, being interested in class discussions, and conscientiously going about any tasks set. He once predicted to me that a young man graduating number 92 in a class of 93 would set the woods on fire and he did. When Jesus said his yoke was easy and his burden light (Matt 11:30), we can perhaps reflect on how he went about his carpentry business, trying to ensure a good fit of the yokes that he made to the back of the animal that would have to wear them. A Christian should be as good at their job as they can be, not to please men or seek praise, but to serve God. St. Paul exhorted the slaves in his congregations to serve their masters well, not to receive a reward from them, but to please Christ and hope that when their masters saw how they conducted themselves they might be led to their Lord. And this is not an extravagant hope. A Christian doing a difficult or boring task as a vocation is a very impressive thing. A former head coach of the Campbell University basketball team was drawn to the Lord by the bearing and behavior of a largely uneducated Christian man who looked after the equipment. One twin, who attended our church in Belfast, was very bright and talented, and he eventually came to faith by observing how his twin brother (a typical second twin perhaps in that he was not as well-endowed academically but a faithful Christian) carried out a rather lowly and unrewarding job in the same building. Our ordinary work is an important means of grace to us and to others.

And fourth, one last topic relating to the Christian life is *sanctification*, the battle against sin in our lives. We are saved *in our sins*, we come as we are, but though that is the vital first step, it is not the end of the matter. We must also deal with the mess remaining in our lives and be saved *from* our sins. This matter is known as sanctification or *holiness*. Holiness is not a popular term. It calls up images that can be less than appealing which we might characterize as sanctimoniousness. But again and again in the New Testament we are called to live righteous lives and to progress in good living both for our own good and to commend our faith to outsiders.

There are two views to consider about sanctification. The commonest is that we slowly and gradually advance day by day and only finally achieve our goal in heaven. The other is that there is an important stage in our spiritual growth when we commit ourselves totally to God. And this latter idea is linked with John Wesley's doctrine of perfection which I'll turn to next in this chapter. Whichever view we take though of this matter the search for godly living is important. We must all go on to deal with the sin that remains in our lives and press on to final salvation.

John Wesley's Doctrine of Christian Perfection

John Wesley taught that it was possible to live sinless in this life. He has received, and still in fact receives, much stick for this opinion. But when we look at what he actually said more carefully, we find that it was less drastic than might appear at first sight. He taught that when we begin our Christian pilgrimage we have only the vaguest idea of the mess that still exists in our lives. Time and further experience and increases in knowledge both of the faith and of ourselves are needed to make us aware of just how much remains to be done. This process commonly leads to a crisis point, a moment of decision to deal with sin seriously. Wesley called this a second experience of grace. He illustrated it from the lives of the patriarchs, Abraham and Jacob. God called Abraham the first time to get out from his kindred and from his father's house and journey to an unknown place. But later God spoke to him a second time, calling him to walk righteously before him. (Gen 17:1).[3] Similarly Jacob first encountered God in the dream he had when he was fleeing from the wrath of his brother Esau. He saw a ladder reaching up to Heaven and the

---

[3] Indeed the call was to be perfect before God.

angels of God ascending and descending on it (Gen 28:10–19). God became real to him, and he made a bargain with God that if he got safely to Haran and eventually returned to his father's house in peace, then the Lord should be his God. Years later, as he was returning home, still mortally afraid of the reception he would meet from Esau, he had a second encounter with God, in the form of a night long wrestling match (Gen 32:20–32) where his nature was changed; he was given a new name *Israel* (God wrestles) and his whole personality seemed to change along with it.

   Wesley spells out what this second experience of grace means in his standard sermon on the text "Be ye also perfect as your father in heaven is perfect (Matt 5:48). In asking what this implies he comments that at the very least it means that we should and can be free from active voluntary sin, for as St. Paul said "sin shall not have dominion over you since you are not under the law but under grace (Rom 6:14). Thus far most would agree although perhaps be concerned that we might fall off the wagon now and then. Wesley calls this being perfect in love, and also "being filled with the spirit" and compares it to the love of a little child which, although a total commitment at the time, has a long way to go. So it is with Christian perfection. It is perfect love so far as that is possible at the time, but with a long way to go in the understanding of the world and of oneself. Though we still may have innumerable faults and much to learn, we can be perfected in love, wishing for nothing but the Father's will. But this is followed by a lifetime of further learning and maturing. Charles Wesley had a two verse hymn about this, and the second verse begins, "But when the work is done, the work is just begun", and states that it will only be complete when we see the face of Jesus in heaven. However, Wesley believed that this gradual sanctification only proceeded apace following total commitment. Wesley encouraged his people to testify to it when they had received this "second blessing". Some did, including the saintly Rector of Madely, John Fletcher. But John Wesley never did make this claim for himself. Indeed it would be difficult to imagine anyone who constantly re-examined himself critically, as he did, making such a claim. He could easily understand the hesitations of his critics but felt obliged to teach what he believed Christ had taught.

Wesley was very much concerned with the need to grow in grace, he called this pressing on to final salvation, but felt that this only proceeded apace following complete commitment to Christ. But however we view sanctification, this desire and search for holiness is a mighty part of our task as Christians. Wesley believed that the Methodist Church was raised up to spread scriptural holiness throughout the land. He was fond of the text, "This is the will of God even your sanctification." (1 Thess 2:4) We are treated as saints by God when he receives us, but we are then called to *be* saints (Rom 1:7).

But there is one very important thing to be remembered here. Being saint-like does not mean feeling saint-like. The most saintly persons generally feel it seems that they fall far short of the mark most of the time. Jesus said, "When you have done all say to yourselves we are unprofitable servants." (Luke 17:10).

The Book of Common Prayer gives thanks for "the means of grace and the hope of glory." The latter is one of the topics of the next chapter.

The Teaching of Jesus—The Beatitudes

The Sermon on the Mount, found in chapters five to seven in St. Matthew's gospel, represent Jesus' review of the Law of Moses. The beatitudes would then seem to occupy the same position as the Ten Commandments which is as a prologue setting forth the general principles that would introduce and guide the instructions that followed.

The beatitudes have been the subject of many sermons and books, but both have commonly failed to consider what their meaning was likely to have been to the original Jewish hearers. The following notes are inspired and spring from Dr. Newton Flew's account of the beatitudes which I heard as a student in a series of lectures which he delivered to the combined Presbyterian and Methodist theological students in Belfast.[4]

---

[4] Later released as *Jesus and His Way: A Study of the Ethics of the New Testament*. London: Epworth, 1963. This piece was published posthumously and edited by one of his former students, but it somehow lacked he punch of the original lectures

Flew's exposition of the beatitudes is based on the rabbinical teachings found in the Mishnah and especially in that part known as the sayings of the fathers (*pirke aboth*). The original hearers, he considers, would have been familiar with the rabbinical teachings, at least in general outline, and understood the teachings of Jesus in these terms.[5]

The first beatitude is "blessed are the poor in spirit for theirs is the kingdom of God." This has been commonly read as a blessing on those who feel that they are spiritually poor, i.e. have no great merit to commend them before God. This is no doubt our condition but it is more likely to have meant something else to a Jewish audience in the first century. The rabbinical literature, according to Dr. Flew, distinguishes several types of poor person. There are the unfortunate poor who are to be helped, the idle poor who are to be shown the door, and finally the spiritual poor who are poor *because* of their loyalty to God. This final type would include those who suffered in the days of the Maccabees when to be a loyal Jew spelled privation and harsh suffering. Another such example would be a rabbinical student who sold even his patrimony, the land that had descended in his family since the days of Joshua, in order to be able to study the Law for seven years. Such a person might well answer the commiserations of their friends by saying that they had chosen the true riches. In short this beatitude is in line with the parable of the man who sold everything in order to purchase the field in which he had found hidden treasure. So blessed is the one who knows what true wealth is and how it is to be found.

The second beatitude is "blessed are the mourners for they shall be comforted." Mourning is a common event in the world over, where the afflicted and all their friends weep and cry out and generally carry on following the death of a loved one or some other such disaster. It is customary for friends and relations to do their part in the mourning, and mourners may even be hired to make a more impressive funeral. Mourning has therefore often been treated with some skepticism.[6] This beatitude blesses the

---

[5] Jesus talking to the elders in the temple (Luke 3:42–50) shows that he was encountering rabbinical teaching.
[6] An old Irish folk song goes "Look at the mourners, ruddy great hypocrites"

true mourner, the sympathetic person who truly feels for those suffering and weeps with those who weep. They themselves will be comforted by God in their own distresses.

The third beatitude is "blessed are the meek (*praus* in Greek, *anav* in Hebrew) for they shall inherit the earth"[7]. To be considered meek in our culture is hardly a compliment ("he's a meek little man") but the term is quite different in the Bible. Moses was described as he meekest of men (Num 12:3): but it was not because he was insignificant or weak. Woe betide you if he found that you had disobeyed the commands of God. Moses was strong for God but he was not concerned about himself and how he was treated. When the Israelites had transgressed horribly and got into God's bad books, Moses prayed that his name be blotted from God's book but that they should be spared. Also when others were prophesying without his authority he did not feel threatened but wished that all the Lord's people were prophets (Num 11:9). Similarly Jesus described himself as meek and lowly in heart (Matt 11:30), not because he was insignificant or weak but that he did not consider his own interests but was willing to lay down his life for the sheep.

The fourth beatitude is "blessed are they that hunger and thirst after righteousness for they shall be filled. The background of his saying is almost certainly the evangel in Isaiah (Is 55:1) "Ho! everyone that thirsts, come to the waters," where what is being sought is righteousness. The Biblical tem "righteousness" (in Hebrew *zedekah*) has no real equivalent in English, and a number of English terms have been used by different translators to express it. As between man and man, it refers to right dealing of every kind. When used of God it is a very active word for it is considering all God's dealings with mankind and includes the notion of salvation, for example, "My righteousness is near, my salvation has gone forth." (Is 51:5) So the most adequate meaning of this beatitude is "happy are they who seek God's salvation, what God can do in their lives, for they will be satisfied."

The fifth beatitude is "blessed are the merciful for they shall obtain mercy". The Hebrew word for mercy is *chesed* and like many

---

[7] The Hebrew *anav* can mean either "humble" or poor"

Hebrew words it is difficult to convey all the nuances of the term in English. For it is a covenant word, implying the obligations of relationships. It covers every kind of good relationship of one person with another especially faithfulness on the part of one of the parties in a binding relationship. In talking of God's righteousness it especially covers His response when the other party to the covenant has broken faith and gone wrong. The supreme example in the Old Testament is found in the prophecy of Hosea who kept buying back his unfaithful wife. The topic of mercy is huge in the Bible. It begins as a characteristic of God who is merciful. He pitied the Israelites in slavery and showed mercy on them by delivering them. And later when thy strayed, and they did so frequently and woefully, He listened to their cries, took pity on them and rescued them Pity is involved in mercy, taking into account and making allowances for the weaknesses of people. It is said that the Lord remembers our frame that we are dust (Ps 103:14). In the Bible, to have mercy is to share one of God's great qualities, to be like our Father in Heaven. And it is a necessary qualification to obtain mercy. Jesus told the parable of the two debtors (Matt 18:23–35), One who had been forgiven an enormous debt by his Lord went out and took one of his fellow workers who owed him a trifling debt by the throat, to squeeze the money out of him. He did not fare well when his Lord heard about it. To be forgiven we must forgive. Why? This parable tells us, it is because we ourselves have been forgiven so much.

The sixth beatitude." Blessed are the pure in heart for they shall see God". The Hebrew term translated pure is *tahor* and it refers to both ceremonial and real cleanliness, as where the psalmist says "create in me a clean heart O God and renew a right spirit within me. (Ps 51) and also in psalm 24 Where it is said "who shall ascend into the hill of the Lord, he that hath clean hands and a pure heart." The context here gives the meaning, the unclean are divided in their loyalties for they worship idols and swear oaths by heathen gods. The clean heart then means the heart undivided in its loyalty to God. This links up with Jesus saying that if your eye is single your whole body will be full of light. The opposite is to be internally divided, being double minded as James puts it (James 1:8). This promise that the pure in heart will see God, clearly means seeing God in the life to come, but we see God in this life also, for Jesus said "He that has seen me has seen the Father (John 14:9). The Pharisees looked at Jesus and saw only a man. When we approach him with undivided heart and receive His spirit we see His glory and see the Father also.

The seventh beatitude. "Blessed are the peacemakers for they shall be called the children of God" The term "children of—" is peculiar in the Bible, it is not just being related to someone but rather being like them: ("like father like son" sort of idea). So some are called children of light, i.e. God's children. Others are called the children of darkness. In the parable of the unjust steward Jesus commended the rascally steward for his shrewd behavior (not for his morals) and commented that the children of this world are wiser in their own generation than the children of light (Luke 16:8). And the peace makers are God's children, for the very nature of God is to bring peace. Peace to the Greeks and Romans of the ancient world was the absence of war and he suppression of violence. In the bible peace (*shalom* in Hebrew) is a much deeper notion, rooted and grounded in the character of God. It is no longer just a cease-fire, but a real peace where the warring parties are restored to a harmonious relationship. God is the author of this kind of peace. Indeed He is called "the God of peace" (2 Cor 13:9). And people who make peace are therefore His children. And they are priceless. Every community and most churches have children of strife and discord. But they also have the children of peace who are blessed and a blessing.

The eighth beatitude is; "Blessed are they that are persecuted for righteousness sake for theirs is the kingdom of Heaven" This beatitude is most apt in ages of persecution, as in the early Roman Empire, in communist Russia, or in Moslem countries where extremists burn churches and murder Christians, But it also applies in everyday life. Christians living in obedience to the beatitudes and doing good to their neighbors can somehow arouse the antipathy of their non-Christian associates who will find all sorts of ways, in small matters or larger, to vent their displeasure on them. But we are told by Jesus to rejoice and be exceeding glad for so persecuted they the prophets who were before you. (Matt 5:11) In this spirit the martyrs met death triumphantly, for Jesus had told them not to fear those that kill the body. Likewise they meet tribulation as a friend, and suffering as a means of grace and a way of showing their faith to all around them. As St Paul says (Rom 5:3) "we glory in tribulation for tribulation produces patience and patience experience and experience hope and our hope is not an empty one."

SUGGESTIONS FOR FURTHER READING

Sangster, W. E. *God Does Guide Us*. New York: Abingdon, 1934. Print. An excellent little guidebook on the Christian life.

Sangster, W. E. *The Path to Perfection: An Examination and Restatement of John Wesley's Doctrine of Christian Perfection*. New York: Abingdon-Cokesbury, 1943. Print.

Arthur, William. *The Tongue of Fire*. New York: Harper & Bros., 1880. Print. This piece again merits mentioning here.

Brother Lawrence. *The Practice of the Presence of God*. United States: Popular Classics, 2012. Print.

Wesley, John. *Christian Perfection*. Cleveland, OH: World, 1954. Print.

XI

Thinking about the Last Things

Certain topics such as death and what follows it, the end of earth as we know it, and the great day of judgment, are all lumped together often under the title of "the last things." These topics have been a subject of great interest and equally of great puzzlement to Christians from Biblical times up to the present. They also make us somewhat apprehensive and, like all frightening things, we tend to push them under the rug, or make them the subject of jokes. In short we only refer to them obliquely and lightly in hope of making them more agreeable and less disturbing. But they need to be faced squarely and honestly.

Of course, this is not an easy task. The great John Calvin wrote a commentary on every book in the Bible except for the Revelation of St. John. He gave up on it saying that he simply couldn't understand it. But these topics are inescapable. Death comes to us all, and we no longer think that our universe is eternal and indestructible; so we have to take our heads out of the sand and think about them. The items of interest I'll pursue here are:

1. The possibility and nature of life after death.
2. The second coming of Christ and the end of the age.
3. The reward of the righteous and the fate of the rest.
4. The new heaven and earth, what the world will look like when it is finally fixed.

1. *Life after death.*

When we look at someone who has passed away we see a dead body. Life is over and we do not see any sign of the beginning of a new existence. Life beyond the grave is admittedly not a thing we experience. It is a matter of faith. But faith is not just a blind hope, it requires a thoughtful basis if it is to be taken as real. What reason then, do we have to think that there is still hope for us beyond the grave? The argument proceeds in several stages.

First, belief in life beyond the grave depends on belief in God, which in turn has a rational basis as we saw at the start of our endeavors here in this volume. Belief in God rests for a start on the idea that the whole creation, including ourselves, cannot be explained away as an accidental happening. The odds against this are astronomical, it requires intelligent design and thinking as we've done throughout in a lateral or horizontal fashion allows us to conclude that God is the cause of it all.

Second, what sort of a being is God? Some scientists and philosophers who have abandoned the idea of an accidental creation and opted for intelligent design, have been quick to dissociate themselves from belief in the God of the Bible. But what kind of designer would have produced beings such as human persons, if not to have fellowship with someone of His own kind. In other words the creator of persons is very unlikely to be a great insect or be anything short of *personal*. The book of Genesis expresses this idea by representing God strolling with Adam and Eve and conversing with them in the cool of the evening; fellowship of like with like.

Third, is it consistent with this purpose, to create beings such as ourselves that only flourish for a little while and then cease to exist? Hardly. As the old poem has it:

Thou wilt not leave us in the dust,
Thou madest man he knows not why,
He thinks he was not made to die
And Thou has made him, Thou art just.

But this brings us to another question. How are we to describe this immortal part or aspect of our humanity that survives death? It has been common to describe it as the *soul*, and to think that when the body dies, it pops out and flies away to a better land. This notion owes a great deal to the influence on our culture of the classical Greek philosophers. They considered the mind, the thinking part, to be much more important than the mere machinery of the body. They were also impressed by the ability of the mind to leave the body, for instance in dreams. And since the mind can exist without the body, it is only a short step to say that it does not die with the body but is immortal. The philosopher Empedocles is said to have jumped into the volcano Etna when it was erupting, in order to prove this point. The poem celebrating this event runs:

> Empedocles, that ardent soul,
> Jumped into Etna and was roasted whole.

Socrates in his dialogue the *Phaedo*, taught that the soul is a prisoner in the earthly body and that death is a liberation, as when a bird flies from a cage; an event to be desired not feared. This view of our human nature, called by its philosophical critics, the "ghost in the machine" has haunted Christian thinking ever since. For a start it is significantly different from the Biblical view of man which is holistic, not divided into separable parts. And there are other puzzlers; one being raised by the modern possibility that someone who has suffered a cardiac arrest and presumably died can now be brought back to life. What happened to their soul in between death and resuscitation? Was it hovering round waiting to be invited back into the body?

The Hebrew notion, largely lost to us when the Biblical traditions were obscured by Greek culture, does not separate soul and body as distinct entities, but rather regards our being as a unity. It has various components with different functions and aspects, but it is one composite entity. Furthermore, although thinking is important in the Bible, it is not the only non-physical function of man, and it is conceived moreover, not as speculative thinking, but as wisdom, which is tied up with thinking about God and God's law. The word translated "soul" in the Old Testament (*nephesh*) was not the platonic mind but the principle of life. It really means "breath." It is what keeps us alive. In Genesis it is said that "God breathed into his (Adam's) nostrils the breath of life and man became a living soul." (Gen 2:7) When the Old Testament writers wish to speak of a more divine aspect of human nature they use the term "*ruach*" (spirit) which refers to the winds that blow, especially the destructive desert storms. The spirit of God is described in these terms, as powerful and blowing when and where it chooses (see John 3:8). Likewise the Divine principle in man is called Spirit. And this does not survive death separate from the body, but is rather reincorporated into a different body, a heavenly one. When St. Paul was describing this process he used the analogy of the seed and the flower. The seed has a body suitable for it to live in the earth, the flower requires a different body to live above ground in the air (1 Cor 15:38–40). So man in the future life to come receives something like a spiritual body which allows him to live in the spiritual world.

The idea of life after death did not arrive in the Bible full grown. There is a progression of thought on this question. Death is early on described as a sleep, but this is not a complete cessation of all existence, sleep itself is hardly that. But in the time of Samuel and Saul it was thought of as a ghostly kind of existence in the house of the dead, which was called *Sheol*, often represented as the grave, the realm of the dead. This word is inaccurately translated as "hell" in the Authorized Version of the Bible. Hell is more properly named *Gehenna, (the valley of Hinnom)* the rubbish heap outside Jerusalem. When the witch of Endor called up the prophet Samuel out of *Sheol* to tell Saul what was going to happen in the ensuing battle, Samuel seemed to be annoyed at being disturbed (1 Sam 25:3–28) This ghostly existence was not deemed especially enjoyable, quite the reverse, for it was said "better to be a live dog than a dead lion" (Ecclesiastes 9:4). But by the period in between the Testaments the waiting state is seen as less ghostly. It was thought that the faithful righteous and the ungodly should not wait for the resurrection in the same place, and that their circumstances should not be the same. So *Sheol* was divided into two parts: the good part, called *Abraham's bosom* was a supremely happy place, and the other part, more or less nameless, is where the unrighteous wait in misery. This arrangement is found in Jesus' parable of the rich man and Lazarus (Luke 16:19–31). The rich man, in torment, asked that Lazarus, who was in Abraham's bosom, might be allowed to come and pour a little water on his tongue to cool it, but he was told that between him and Lazarus there was a great gulf fixed.

So while the New Testament, and Jesus Himself continues to speak of a final resurrection of the dead at the end of the age, life immediately after death for the righteous is described essentially as Christians depict it, as "being with Christ which is far better."

(Phil 1:23)

2. The Great Day of Judgment.

The Old Testament taught that on a certain day, the day of the Lord, the graves would open and the dead would be raised again to be judged according to their works. When Jesus, after Lazarus' death, said to his sister Martha that Lazarus would live again, Martha replied that she knew that he would rise again on the last day (John 11:24). St Paul, indeed, describes this event in some detail, saying that when Christ returns, a trumpet will sound and the dead would be raised incorruptible (1 Cor 15:32), some to eternal life and others to punishment. Paul goes on to say that at Christ's return in glory, the faithful dead would be raised first and then the disciples who had survived alive would be taken up to meet the returning Lord in the air (Thess 4:14–17). Jesus himself seems to have taught a resurrection of the dead for judgment on the last day. In the parable of the wheat and the tares, both were allowed to grow together till the harvest when the difference between them would be more obvious. The wheat would then be gathered into the storehouses and the tares bundled and burned (Matt 13:24–30). And this waiting period before the great judgment is still often compared to sleep. Jesus said that Lazarus was not dead but asleep (John 11:11).

Somewhat different from these passages are those where Jesus, and Paul, seem to say that immediately on death, the faithful are "with the lord." So Jesus says to Martha, "I am the resurrection and the life, he that believes in me, though he were dead, yet shall he live and whoever being alive believes in me shall never die." (John 11:25–26) Similarly on the cross Jesus said to the repentant thief, "Today you shall be with me in paradise." (Luke 23:43) Paul for his part says that to be absent from the body was to be present with the Lord (2 Cor 5:8). These passages seem to say, as most Christians believe, that on leaving this life, they will be with Christ, which is in essence being in Heaven. These somewhat difficult sayings can be harmonized when we take into account the Jewish notion of Abraham's bosom which was also referred to as Paradise. But there is another more serious problem.

On the great judgment day, when the books are opened and all our doings are brought to light, the outcome seems to be decided on the basis of our deeds, balancing good against bad. So in the parable of the sheep and the goats (Matt 25:31–46) on the last day, the sheep are divided from the goats and judgment is provided according to their works. This seems to run counter to the general teaching of the New Testament that salvation cannot be purchased by good works but depends instead on faith. The Jews of Jesus' time sought to be saved by doing the works of God, which they identified with keeping the Mosaic commandments. Jesus indeed said that by keeping the commandments the Pharisees would live (Luke 10:28).[1] But Jesus also reinterpreted the works of God as believing in the One whom He has sent (John 6:29). Likewise the writer of the Johannine letters who constantly emphasize keeping God's commandments, go on to say that, "this is His commandment that we believe in Him whom He has sent." (1 John 3:23)

Jesus also said that anyone who believed in him should not come under judgment but has passed from death into life. (John 5: 24). This opens another avenue of thought on the great Day of Judgment. It would seem to imply that the true believer will not come into the general judgment of mankind but will have, so to speak, a yellow brick road to eternal life. On the other hand, the generality of mankind who have not encountered the Christ to accept or reject Him, will be judged by their deeds, presumably to see whether they would have accepted Christ if they had been given the chance. Another way of dealing with the problem of faith and works on the great Day of Judgment is to say that it is not us but our works that are judged. So while our salvation depends on accepting Christ, our works which we have built on this foundation, will be tested by fire, and may come to nothing though we ourselves may be saved (1 Cor 3:15).

Different Christian writers approach these matters in different ways and all these texts are theological battle grounds with shell holes and burning buildings all over the place. So how are we to position ourselves in the midst of all this theory and controversy?

---

[1] This may have been a tongue in cheek remark since He knew that no one could in fact do that solely on their own efforts.

First, it is important to remember what the controversy is about. It concerns future events, which are always difficult to imagine in advance.[2] The Jews accepted the prophesies of the coming of the Messiah but failed to recognize Him when he arrived. We must plant our feet where the ground is surest, that is in the very words of Christ, the pivotal point of all Revelation. And the central point here must be that of John 11 where he said that whoever believed in Him would never die but have eternal life.

Another problem relates to the interpretation of death as sleep. The notion that we sleep till judgment day is very repulsive to some people. A lot depends on how we view sleep. J. Agar Beet in his monumental work on the last things, points out that sleep is by no means a cessation of experience. The paradise mentioned by Jesus in his words to the dying thief on the cross, was the term used to describe the great pleasure park of the Persian kings. So the sleep of death can be seen as a joyous waiting for the final summation of all things in the presence of Christ.

3. *The Return of Christ and the End of All Things.*

The Bible teaches that there will be an end to existence as we know it on the return of Christ. The general idea seems to be that the world as we know it will perish, the stars in the heavens will fall, and the heavens themselves be rolled up like a scroll (Rev 6:13-14). These sayings at one time seemed very foreign to us, as the earth, the sun and all the parts of our universe have always appeared to be very stable and likely to last for ever. More recent knowledge has made us feel less secure. Our earth, seemingly once safe, is really a very dangerous place, with volcanoes, tidal waves, pestilences and other horrors abounding. Volcanoes, indeed, are not so far away as we thought, for great clouds of gas emanating from them can block the sunlight thousands of miles away and bring an ice age upon us. The tiny meteors which strike the earth miss most of us but what of bigger ones that are floating around us. One of these may have wiped out almost the entire

---

[2] J. Agar Beet, mighty Methodist theologian of the early twentieth century in his book *The Last Things* (London: Hodder and Stoughton, 1905) stresses this point in relation to the end time events generally

race of animals then extant. There is even the possibility of much larger comets, even up to the size of the moon, wiping us all out. A couple of these have already given us a near miss and some estimate an even closer shave, possibly a direct hit, may occur in the future. The sun itself, the source of all life in our solar system, could become a red giant and render earth and all on it extinct. Beams of gamma rays emanating from certain kinds of dying small suns could also wipe us all out. In short the universe is much more apocalyptic than we thought. Some have suggested that the only hope for mankind is to develop intergalactic travel to some distant sun with planets that might hold an atmosphere and allow life as we know it to continue. This does not seem a serious option and even if it could be managed, only a tiny minority of humanity could make the long and hazardous journey. It is difficult to imagine us booking seats for such a flight.

It is better for us to realize that in God's good time there will be an end to history and that in the meantime, like Noah, we should be building an ark, not a space ship but being ready to meet the end when it comes. As Jesus commentary on the parable of the wise and foolish virgins puts it, blessed are those servants who will be found awake and alert when He comes. And the ark should not be just for our family and friends but for all mankind: for it is not the will of your Father in Heaven that any should perish but that all should come to repentance (2 Pet 3:9). So we need to intensify our missionary efforts.

4. *The New Jerusalem.*

The Old Testament speaks of the Kingdom of God where God will reign and put an end to all evil. This thought is taken up in the New Testament where the Kingdom of God is an important part of Christ's teaching. This idea is most elaborately expressed in the vision of the New Jerusalem descending from heaven like as a bride adorned for her husband (Rev 21 and 22). The walls and foundations here are of precious stones and the door of each of the twelve gates is a single large pearl. There is no need for city lights for the Lord is the light. And a river runs out of the city, the river of life, with trees on either side that yield a different fruit each month with leaves that are for the healing of the nations. The righteous who have followed the lamb will be allowed within the city and the wicked will be left outside.

What will this restoration of God's will be like, when Christ's kingdom comes and his will is finally done? Many ideas, often bizarre, have been put forward. Basically the city is described as being too wonderful for words. The things deemed most precious among us now are used as paving stones and building foundations in the New Jerusalem. Going beyond this, interpreting in more realistic terms, some have thought that it will be an earthly kingdom with all the garbage cleared up and the creation as it was meant to be, restored. Some have even thought that this would take place on a different planet that we haven't messed up yet. The most common opinion is that it refers to heaven, the place where God already reigns supreme. J Agar Beet again reminds us that prophesy is one thing, fulfillment another. St. Paul likewise reminds us that eye has not seen nor the ear heard nor has I entered into the heart of man the things that God has prepared for those that love Him (1 Cor 2:9).

The question of the fate of the wicked and ungodly is also hotly debated. It has commonly been argued that their lot is eternal or at least very prolonged torture. Since the Devil himself is due to be finally destroyed in the lake of fire, presumably the lost will share his fate. Different authors have proposed a number of alternatives. One is *universalism*, the idea that the punishment is reformative resulting in eventual salivation for all. This is deemed a little optimistic by most. Another is that though the righteous are raised to eternal life, the rest are simply not raised and so perish. J. Agar Beet was thought to advocate this and persecuted somewhat for it by his ultra conservative brethren. But that was not what he said. His point was that the scriptures are to a large extent silent or inconclusive on these and many other questions and that we should not go beyond what is written. And this seems sound advice. What should we take from the teaching of the Bible generally and from Jesus in particular on these difficult and obscure matters?

1. That God has sent his Son to bring us back to Him and

that it is a very serious matter indeed to refuse his call.

2. That Christ's Kingdom, though not of this world and not brought in by force, is nevertheless real. Like seed in the ground it is growing and will grow to conquer evil.

3. That God's rule is quiet, again like seed growing in the ground (Mark 4:26). And this must be so for if God openly showed His hand, rewarding good and thumping evil as they occurred, we would all be rendered good by force, but God wants children not machines, real goodness and not reflex conditioned behavior.

4. The ultimate end of all things can be looked for and hoped for, but its time and manner are unimaginable at present. In the meantime, however, the battles between Good and Evil, depicted in the Book of Revaluation are with us here and now, with the Devil and his angels constantly being defeated but then regrouping for another attempt to defeat God's purposes. So we must be prepared to live with one battle following another till the final great battle arrives.

5. The nature of God's final victory is given to us in glowing symbolic terms which are often difficult to interpret in the here and now. But in the meantime we can look forward to being with Christ in Heaven where God rules supreme and it is in His presence that our true treasure and fulfillment lies.

Mr. Wesley remarked that our people die well. If our hope lies in these things we will surely both live and die well.

SUGGESTIONS FOR FURTHER READING

Beet, Joseph Agar. *The Last Things*. London: Hodder and Stoughton, 1905. Print. A careful and extensive review of Biblical teaching on this topic.

Oesterley, W. O. E. *The Doctrine of the Last Things Jewish and Christian*. London: John Murray, 1908. Print. A scholarly review of Jewish apocalyptic sources that lay behind the New Testament teaching on the end times.

Notes

www.ingramcontent.com/pod-product-compliance
Lightning Source LLC
Chambersburg PA
CBHW071709040426
42446CB00011B/1983